OSCAR WILDE
A LIFE IN LETTERS, WRITINGS AND WIT

Oscar Wilde

A Life in Letters, Writings and Wit

Juliet Gardiner

C&B

COLLINS & BROWN

First published in Great Britain in 1995
by Collins & Brown Limited
London House
Great Eastern Wharf
Parkgate Road
London SW11 4NQ

British Library Cataloguing-in-Publication Data:
A catatlogue record for this book is available from the British Library.

ISBN: 1 85585 205 5 (hardback edition)
ISBN: 1 85585 242X (paperback edition)

Conceived, designed and edited by Collins & Brown Limited
Editor: Catherine Bradley
Art Director: Roger Bristow
Designer: Ruth Prentice
Picture Research: Philippa Lewis

Reproduction by Master Image PTE Ltd
Printed and bound inSpain

FRONT COVER: *(from right to left):*
*Portrait of Oscar Wilde by Henri de
Toulouse-Lautrec, 1895; Letter from Oscar
Wilde; Photograph of Oscar Wilde;
Programme for the first performance of* The
Importance of Being Earnest *14
February 1895; Detail from American trade
card showing Oscar Wilde at the time of his
lecture tour.*

BACK COVER: *Detail from*
A Private View at the Royal Academy
by W.P.Frith, 1881.

FRONTISPIECE:
*Danse de la Goulue by Henri de
Toulouse-Lautrec (Wilde is the second
figure from the left).*

Contents

INTRODUCTION

'And I?' Oscar Wilde had said from the dock of the Old Bailey on 25 May 1895, 'May I say nothing…?' But Mr Justice Wills waved aside the interruption and 'the most brilliant talker, the most witty, the most audacious' personality of *fin de siècle* London was led down in silence to begin a sentence of two years' hard labour for acts of gross indecency.

> *And never a human voice comes near*
> *To speak a gentle word*
> *And the eye that watches through the door*
> *Is pitiless and hard.*
>
> (The Ballad of Reading Gaol)

'The dinner table was Wilde's event and made him the greatest talker of all time, and his plays and his dialogues have what merit they possess from being now an imitation, now a record, of his talk,' summed up Wilde's fellow Irishman, the poet and dramatist W.B. Yeats. 'I had never before heard a man talking with perfect sentences, as if he had written them all overnight with labour, and yet all spontaneous.' The writer André Gide reflected that 'Wilde did not converse, he narrated,' and those sentences, that narration (written and spoken), were the mark of a natural wordsmith revelling in the possibilities and paradoxes of language. The same quality of immediacy, characterized by humorous or astringent asides, dominates his letters to a wide range of recipients: lovers, friends, family, actor/managers, newspaper and magazine editors, admirers and detractors. It is from this multifarious correspondence, as well as the outpouring of plays, stories, articles and essays, that this telling of Wilde's life derives.

INTRODUCTION

'I hope you will enjoy my 'trivial' play,' Wilde had written of *The Importance of Being Earnest,* which opened at the Haymarket Theatre on 14 February 1895. 'It is written by a butterfly for butterflies.' Wilde, the less than ideal husband, did not understand – or chose not to understand – the importance of being earnest, for it was with his wit that he exposed and challenged Victorian society. He proved a formidable opponent. His epigrams inverted commonplaces and lanced hypocrisies. His aestheticism was ridiculed and yet in its spectacle, intellectual rigour and homo-eroticism, it confronted, and became a slow-burning fuse within, a society grown stale in art as in morality. 'How strange to live in a land where the worship of beauty and the passion of love are considered infamous. I hate England,' Wilde had written to Lord Alfred Douglas in November 1894. 'It is only bearable because you are here.'

Earlier in the year that he went to prison, two of Wilde's plays (*An Ideal Husband* and *The Importance of Being Earnest*) had opened in the West End within little more than a month of one another. Critical acclaim for both plays capped his earlier successes, *A Woman of No Importance* and *Lady Windermere's Fan*. Praise was heaped upon Wilde's theatrical skill and the perfection of his dialogue. The *New York Times* was led to conclude that 'Oscar Wilde may be said to have at last, and by a single stroke, put his enemies under his feet'. But less than three months later his enemies seemed to tower. The *Daily Telegraph* pontificated on his conviction:

> No sterner rebuke could well have been inflicted on some of the artistic tendencies of the time than the condemnation of Oscar Wilde…the man has

LEFT: *'From Aesthete to Convict (Our Captious Critic)': A sequence of cartoons reviewing Oscar Wilde's lecture tour of America from* The Illustrated Sporting and Dramatic News, *21 July 1882. It anticipates with astonishing dramatic irony the events of Wilde's later life.*

INTRODUCTION

now suffered the penalties of his career, and may well be allowed to pass from that platform of publicity which he loved into that limbo of disrepute and forgetfulness which is his due. The grave of contemptuous oblivion may rest on his foolish ostentation, his empty paradoxes, his insufferable posturing, his incurable vanity'.

But the resonance of his words and the recollection of his life have ensured that no blanket of oblivion has settled on Oscar Wilde in the hundred years since that judgement. 'He has become the symbolic figure of his age,' pronounced the poet, Richard Le Gallienne, many years after his friend's death.

'I have my put my genius into my life and only my talent into my works,' Wilde explained to André Gide. Yet the fascination of the two is their synergy. When he supplied a volume of his poetry to the Oxford Union, Wilde suffered the humiliation of having it rejected as the poetry of a plagiarist. But if he recklessly plundered anyone's work, it was his own. Unable to resist his own telling phrases and witty formulations, he re-worked them in his conversation, his letters, his poems and his plays.

The protean and enduring quality of Wilde's writing, and in particular of his letters – written in love, in anger, in sorrow, but above all in friendship – testify to the truth of the life he told in *De Profundis*:

> The gods had given me almost everything. I had genius, a distinguished name, a high social position, brilliancy, intellectual daring…I altered the minds of men and the colour of things: there was nothing I said or did that did not make people wonder…whatever I touched I made beautiful in a new mode of beauty…I treated Art as the supreme reality, and life as a mere mode of fiction: I awoke the imagination of my century…I forgot that…what one has done in the secret chamber one has someday to cry aloud from the rooftops.

A hundred years on, the words of Oscar Wilde continue to echo ever louder from the rooftops.

CHAPTER 1

'YOUTH HAS A KINGDOM WAITING FOR IT'

'Behold me – me, Speranza – rocking a cradle at this present writing in which lies my second son – a babe of one month old the 16th of this month and as large and fine and handsome and healthy as if he were three months. He is to be called Oscar Fingal Wilde. Is not that grand, misty, and Ossianic?' wrote Jane Francesca Wilde to a friend. In fact, the names finally bestowed on the infant owed even more to the Gaelic bard – and were even grander – than his mother suggested. The second son of 'Speranza' and her husband, William, was born on 16 October 1854 and christened Oscar Fingal O'Flahertie Wills Wilde – a string of appellations, drawn from life and legend, that their owner was to edit for his own purposes in adult life.

> My name has two O's, two F's, and two W's. A name which is destined to be in everybody's mouth must not be too long. It comes so expensive in advertisements. When one is unknown, a number of Christian names are useful, perhaps needful. As one becomes famous, one sheds some of them, just as a balloonist, … rising higher, sheds unnecessary ballast…All but two of my five names have been thrown overboard.[Oscar Fingal remained.] Soon I shall discard another and be known simply as 'The Wilde' or 'The Oscar'.

The flourish of names was to be expected. Mrs Wilde (or Lady Wilde as she became when her husband was knighted in January 1864) was proud to admit that she loved 'to make a sensation' and by the time Oscar was born, his mother was a well-known figure in Dublin society and beyond. She was a patriot, a poet and a presence. Deeply affected by the nationalist poetry of others, particularly Thomas Davis, she had found her own distinctive

ABOVE: *A sketch of the Mound of Douth in Ireland, from* The Beauties of the Boyne and Blackwater *(1850) by Sir William Wilde. Oscar's father was dedicated to the cause of Irish folklore and archaeology.*

LEFT: *Dublin from* The Three Rock Mountain, Co. Dublin *by William Craig, 1849. By 1854 Dublin had lost much of its importance to become 'a deposed capital', with a sharp division between the fine Georgian squares of the south where the Wilde family lived, and the miserable tenements round the River Liffey.*

OSCAR WILDE

voice in verse, which she first submitted to the editor of the *Nation*, Charles Gavan Duffy, in 1846 using the *nom de plume* 'Speranza' (Italian for 'hope'). Speranza's patriotism had made her a poet and her verses, as her prose, were committed to the cause of freeing Ireland from English rule. Her learning was considerable; she was a linguist, capable of 'mastering two European languages before I was eighteen'; an adept translator from Russian, Turkish, Spanish, Italian and Portuguese, who scattered her poetry and prose with Greek and Latin epigrams; and she published thirteen books, including collections of her poetry, Irish myths and legends, and translations, including her best known of Meinhold's *Sidonia the Sorceress*. A statuesque woman, some six feet tall, with handsome aquiline features – which she attributed to having been an eagle in a previous existence – she dressed with flair and flamboyance. 'She is undoubtedly a genius, and won my heart very soon,' confided the brilliant Irish mathematician Sir William Rowan Hamilton in 1845, describing her as 'a very odd and original lady ...She is almost amusingly fearless and original, and averse (though in that, as in other respects) she perhaps exaggerates whatever is unusual about her that she likes to make a sensation...I think she has a noble nature (though a rebellious one)'.

Speranza's second son, Oscar, appreciated his mother all his life. Her unwavering support for him and her unshakeable, frequently expressed belief in his genius were matched by his concern, respect and affection for her. In *The Importance of Being Earnest* he was to lament 'All women become like their mothers. That is their tragedy. No man does. That's his'.

On 14 November 1851 at St Peter's Protestant Church in Dublin, Speranza married William Wilde. The bridegroom was eleven years older than his bride. He was an aural surgeon and oculist, whose name has passed into medical terminology, and who, in 1863, was appointed Surgeon Oculist to the Queen in Ireland – available on the spot should Victoria ever have cause to come to Ireland and need such services. He was innovative in his approach to medicine, travelling around Europe in his

BELOW: A print showing St Mark's Ophthalmic Hospital for Diseases of the Eye and Ear, established by William Wilde in Mark Street, Dublin, in 1844. The hospital grew from humble origins. Wilde converted a stable at home into a dispensary for the poor, run on 'scientific principles' and opposed to the 'shroud of quackery' surrounding medicine at that time.

studies, compiling the incidence of blindness and deafness in Ireland for the census of 1851, and publishing the earliest textbooks in the field of ear and eye surgery. He was reputed to have 'removed the squint from the eye of a British princess when no one else would attempt the operation'. However, when he attempted to do the same for the father of George Bernard Shaw, he succeeded only in enabling Shaw senior to 'squint the other way all the rest of his life'.

William Wilde was also the father of three acknowledged illegitimate children when he married – 'a family in every farmhouse' was George

Bernard Shaw's verdict. Henry Wilson (born in 1838) was to join his father in his medical practice. Emily (1847) and Mary (1849) were both adopted by William's eldest brother, the Reverend Ralph Wilde, and brought up as Wildes until their tragic deaths in 1871 from burns sustained as the one, invited to a ball, pirouetted in her crinoline too close to an open fire, and the other went to her aid. Deaths that were all the more dreadful since the tragedy 'had to be buried in silence'.

Soon three children born in wedlock paralleled the three born outside the institution of marriage. William Charles Kingsbury Wills was born on 26 September 1852; Oscar Fingal O'Flahertie Wills a little over two years later. Both boys owed the name Wills to their cousins, landowners in County Roscommon who numbered the playwright W. G. Wills among the family. William was called for his father, with Kingsbury added in deference to his mother's family. Oscar and Fingal were both taken from Irish legend, Oscar being the name of the son of Ossian, the third-century Irish warrior poet, killed at the battle of Gabhra in single combat with King Cairbre. Fingal was Ossian's father, and also the hero, in Ossian's poems, who delivered Erin from her enemies. The Galway name, O' Flahertie, derived from the 'ferocious O'Flaherties', linked back to William's father's grandmother. On 2 April 1857, the third child, a daughter, was born and christened Isola Francesca. She was soon deemed to have 'fine eyes' and the promise of 'a most acute intellect' by her mother, who added 'These two gifts are enough for any woman'.

William (or Willie as he was known) and Oscar were both born in Dublin at 21 Westland Row. In June 1855 when Oscar was nearly a year old

ABOVE: An illustration showing an ancient tomb in the Royal Cemetery of Brugh na Boinne, from The Beauties of the Boyne and Blackwater *by Sir William Wilde. Oscar's father had a deep love of Ireland and its culture. He compiled* A Descriptive Catalogue of Irish Antiquities *and was awarded the Royal Irish Academy's Cunningham Medal, its highest honour. For those patients unable to pay, he would often barter his medical services for the retelling of ancient folklore and superstitions.*

ABOVE: A portrait of Sir William Wilde by Erskine Nicol, 1854. A respected surgeon and oculist, he was the author of two of the earliest textbooks in the field of opthalmics and his name still describes some medical procedures. He also compiled exhaustive medical statistics for the Irish census of 1851 which revealed the terrible consequences of the 1840s famine.

LEFT: The Seafront at Bray, Co. Wicklow *by Erskine Nicol, 1862. The Wilde family had a house at this seaside resort near Dublin, and it was whilst staying at Bray with Oscar and Willie in May 1864 that Lady Wilde was further harassed by the activities of one Mary Travers. This young Dublin woman published a series of pamphlets lampooning the Wildes as Doctor and Mrs Quilp and alleging that when she was his patient several years before, Sir William had administered chloroform and raped her in his consulting rooms.*

and, according to his mother, 'a great stout creature who minds nothing but growing fat', the family's increasing prosperity allowed them to move up in the world. In later life Oscar was to claim that he had been born at the house they now moved into, complete with the trappings of a French maid, a German governess and six servants. The house, a large Georgian residence with imposing ironwork balconies, had one of Dublin's smartest addresses, 1 Merrion Square.

With its 'fine rooms and the best situation in Dublin', Merrion Square was perfect for entertaining. Speranza's nationalist fervour seemed to have abated after the failure of the 1848 uprisings. 'I take an interest now in children beyond all other objects in life,' she wrote after Oscar's birth. 'Revolutions may agitate and dynasties fall, but I have scarce a thought for them…a woman cannot live for her country and her children.' The Wildes kept a renowned salon. There would be dinner parties and soon gatherings for dozens of guests on a Saturday afternoon, comprising professional colleagues of Sir William, government officials, academics, and any artist, writer or performer who happened to be passing through Dublin. Even though it was daylight, the curtains were kept drawn – Speranza rose late and, even when a young woman, preferred to socialize in the semi-gloom. The boys were often allowed to attend these social occasions, but they had to sit quietly and not speak.

Then, when Oscar was almost ten and Willie was twelve, they were sent away to Portora Royal School at Enniskillen in County Fermanagh – until then the boys had been largely tutored at home.

Perched on a hill overlooking Lough Erne, with a Protestant clergyman, the Reverend William Steele D.D. as its headmaster, Portora was a public school that enjoyed a high academic reputation coupled with relatively reasonable fees of £17 10 shillings a term per pupil. Oscar's considerable ability was obvious from the first – 'I was looked on as a prodigy by my associates,' he told a friend towards the end of his life, '…quite frequently, I would, for a wager, read a three-volume novel in half an hour so closely

ABOVE: *A drawing of the Maiden Tower from* The Beauties of the Boyne and Blackwater *by Sir William Wilde. When the great historian Macaulay was writing his history of England, and came to inspect the site of the Battle of the Boyne, it was William Wilde who was his guide.*

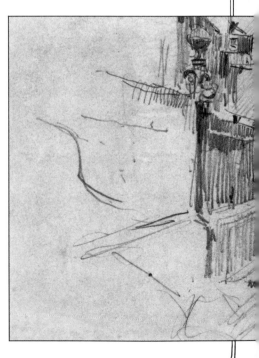

'YOUTH HAS A KINGDOM WAITING FOR IT'

as to be able to give an accurate *résumé* of the plot of the story: by one hour's reading I was enabled to give a fair narrative of incidental scenes and the most pertinent dialogue.' Speranza was soon boasting: 'Willie is all right, but as for Oscar, he will turn out something wonderful.' Oscar's literary and aesthetic inclinations were evident in a letter he wrote home dated September 1868:

> Darling Mama, The hamper came today, and I never got such a jolly surprise, many thanks for it, it was more than kind of you to think of it. Don't please forget to send me the National Review…The flannel shirts you sent in the hamper are both Willie's, mine are one scarlet and the other lilac but it is too hot to wear them yet. You never told me anything about the publisher in Glasgow, what does he say? And have you written to Aunt Warren on the green note paper?

He also enclosed a drawing captioned 'ye delight of ye boys at ye hamper and ye sorrow of ye hamperless boy'. Unsurprisingly, Wilde had little interest in games at school, 'I never liked to kick or be kicked', though 'nearly everyone went in for athletics – running and jumping and so forth…No one appeared to care for sex. We were healthy young barbarians and that was all. Knowledge came to me through pleasure, as it always comes, I imagine.'

Wilde found this transfixing pleasure at Portora when he became absorbed in his lifetime affair with antiquity. 'I was nearly sixteen when the wonder and beauty of the old Greek life began to dawn upon me…I began to read Greek eagerly, and the more I read the more I was enthralled.' One of the masters at Portora was a Mr J.F. Davies who, in 1866, had published an edition with commentary of Aeschylus' *Agamemnon*. Wilde was caught up with its literary resonances and read deeper into Greek and Latin texts, translating them orally with such facility that he easily beat the boy who was later to become a distinguished professor of Latin at Trinity College at a *viva voce* on the *Agamemnon*. In 1870 he won the Carpenter prize for

BELOW: A sketch of Merrion Row, Dublin by Walter Frederic Osberne. With its 'fine rooms and the best situation in Dublin', 1 Merrion Square, where the Wildes moved in 1855, was perfect for Speranza's role as a hostess to Dublin society – and to any interesting artist, writer or poet who happened to be visiting the city.

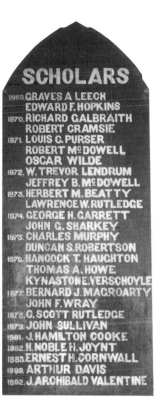

ABOVE: The roll of honour at Portora Royal School where Oscar Wilde was a pupil from 1864–71. When he won a scholarship to Trinity College, Dublin Wilde's name was emblazoned on the board. When he was sent to prison it was erased. Now restored, the gilt letters stand a little proud of those above and below.

Oscar Wilde

Greek testament and the following year was one of three pupils awarded a Portora Royal School scholarship to Trinity College, Dublin.

However, whilst Oscar was away making a stir, despite his pronounced boredom with school – 'Nothing that is worth knowing can be taught' – there had been a tragedy at home.

Oscar Wilde was twelve when his younger sister Isola, aged nine, died of fever in the spring of 1867. The local doctor who ministered to her – she was staying with an uncle and aunt in the country – described Oscar at the time as 'an affectionate, gentle, retiring dreamy, boy…whose lonely and inconsolable grief found its outward expression in long and frequent visits to his sister's grave in the village cemetery'. Sir William wrote that Isola's death had made him 'a mourner for life'. Lady Wilde tried to find consolation in her remaining children, but it was hard. 'My sons were home for the vacation,' she wrote to her friend, the Swedish writer, Lotten von Kraemer, on black-edged paper, 'fine clever fellows – the eldest quite grown-up looking – I thank God for these blessings. Still a sadness is on me for life – a bitter sorrow that can never be healed.' In 1875 she wrote to condole a bereaved friend: 'I know too well the grief you suffer. Eight years have passed since I, too, stood by a grave – but the sorrow knows no change and sometimes it deepens with the bitterness of despair.'

Oscar Wilde, too, felt diminished by his sister's death. He kept a lock of her hair in an envelope with the words 'My Isola's Hair' and 'She is not dead but sleepeth' written above two linked wreaths, one surrounding an 'O', the other an 'I'. Later, when a young man travelling in France, he wrote a poem, 'Requiescat', expressing his own sense of melancholy at this early loss:

> Tread lightly, she is near
> Under the snow,
> Speak gently, she can hear
> The daisies grow.

LEFT: *A sketch of Sir William and Lady Wilde by Harry Furniss. 'Do you know me?' Sir William is supposed to have asked a fellow member of the British Association in 1874, 'I'm Wilde'. 'By God, you look it,' was the reply, whilst his six-foot wife is reputed to have reprimanded a servant for stacking plates on the coal scuttle, since 'what are the chairs meant for?'*

LEFT: The Four Courts, Dublin *by Walter Osborne. In December 1864, as in 1895, a member of the Wilde family appeared in court over a libel case. In 1864 Mary Travers sued Lady Wilde for libel over a letter Speranza had written to Travers' father. This complained of his daughter's 'disreputable conduct' in disseminating 'tracts in which she makes it appear that she has had an intrigue with Sir William Wilde'. The jury found libel proved, but awarded Miss Travers only a farthing in damages.*

OSCAR WILDE

All her bright golden hair
Tarnished with rust,
She that was young and fair
Fallen to dust…

Peace, Peace, she cannot hear
Lyre or sonnet,
All my life's buried here,
Heap earth upon it.

Trinity College had a high academic reputation for classical scholarship – and one man in particular liked to think of himself as its exemplar. Two years before Oscar Wilde went up, the Reverend J.P. Mahaffy – who had certainly attended one of his mother's salons – had been appointed to its Chair of Ancient History. The thirty-two year old Mahaffy was a considerable polyglot. Apart from his familiarity with classical Greek and Latin he was fluent in German, highly competent in French and Italian and well-versed in Hebrew. For Mahaffy civilization was vested in the Greeks (which he pronounced 'Gweeks'). Wilde was tutored in Latin at Trinity by another fine classicist, Robert Yelverton Tyrrell, who had been appointed Professor of Latin at the young age of twenty-five. Less obviously a man of all talents than the showier Mahaffy, Tyrrell was a kinder man and a more rigorous – if less flamboyant – scholar than his colleague. Wilde was well served. It was at Trinity that, in his mother's words, he received 'the first noble impulse to your intellect that kept you out of the toils of meaner men and pleasures'.

And the pleasures brought rewards. In his first year Wilde could hardly have done better, coming top of those in the first class; in a competitive examination in 1873 he received one of ten highly sought-after Foundation Scholarships, and when he scored the highest mark in a taxing examination on Meineke's *Fragments of the Greek Comic Poets* in 1874, he was awarded the Berkeley Gold Medal for Greek.

RIGHT: *A lithograph of Trinity College, Dublin. Founded in 1592, it is the oldest university in Ireland. Wilde had rooms on the north side 'of one of the older squares, known as Botany Bay [which] were exceedingly grimy and ill-kept'. He never entertained there. When rare visitors were admitted, an unfinished landscape in oils was always on the easel in his sitting room. He would…refer to it…in his humorously unconvincing way [saying] that 'he had just put in the butterfly'.*

Lithographed by Newman. & Co. 48 Watling St. London

OSCAR WILDE

Willie Wilde, who had preceded his brother at Trinity, and who had won a Gold Medal for Ethics, left Ireland for London in 1872 to study law at the Middle Temple. Oscar determined to follow his brother to England. Mahaffy did not discourage him as he was not convinced that Wilde would be offered a fellowship at Trinity on graduation. Sir William, who had become anxious that his younger son was dallying with Catholicism, anticipated that a break with Ireland might effect a desirable rupture with the seductions of Popish ways.

On 23 June 1874 Oscar Wilde presented himself at Magdalen College, Oxford, to sit the examination for one of the two Demyships [scholarships] in classics that the college was offering. Each was worth £95 a year and was tenable for five years. He sat the exam with frequent interruptions to request more paper – his generous hand covered sheet after sheet with spidery writing that only managed to fit in four words to a line. 'One wonders,' pondered a fellow Demy scholar, 'if examiners ever mark by weight.' Again, he came top.

Oscar Wilde found the ancient city of Oxford entirely to his taste – it was 'the most beautiful thing in England' and the three years he spent there were 'the most flower-like time' of his life. It was the interlude which honed his aesthetic taste and temperament. He had rooms in Magdalen on which he spent considerable thought – and a not insubstantial amount of money – equipping them with fine glass for entertaining, candles, ornaments, and most notably a pair of blue Sèvres vases which he filled with the aesthete's favourite flower, the languorous lily. 'I find it harder every day to live up to my blue china' was a widely circulated remark that made him infamous in undergraduate circles where he was to be caricatured as 'O'Flighty'.

Within the small, intense world of Oxford, Wilde soon became both famous and somewhat notorious. 'He was,' recalled one G.T. Atkinson, his fellow Demy scholar, writing in the Cornhill Magazine in 1929, 'a personality from the first':

ABOVE: *The young Wilde at Oxford, 1878. 'The two turning points in my life were when my father sent me to Oxford and when Society sent me to prison,' wrote Wilde in recollection.*

ABOVE: *A cartoon of Wilde in* Punch *as Harold Skimpole, the child-like character in Dickens' Bleak House. Wilde, however, saw his youthful aestheticism rather less whimsically. 'I was a man,' he was to write, 'who stood in symbolic relation to the art and culture of my age. I had realised this for myself at the very dawn of my manhood, and had forced my age to realise it afterwards.*

'YOUTH HAS A KINGDOM WAITING FOR IT'

His hair was much too long, sometimes parted in the middle, sometimes at the side and he tossed it off his face with much the same gesture that is used by the flapper today. His face was colourless, moon-like, with heavy eyes and thick lips: he had a perpetual simper and a convulsive laugh. He swayed as he walked, and lolled when at table. I never saw him run…He came up having read much more than most of us, including all the "fragments" of the Greek dramatists…Of savoir-faire he had abundance, and also of self-conceit. Sincerity was not his strong point; it was 'bourgeois'…Charming rooms were given to him overlooking the Cherwell, and he decorated them lavishly. The usual pictures in the 'seventies were hired at Ryman's, stags crossing a lake, Swiss mountains, or 'sloppy' but innocuous portraits of maidens. Wilde had a more luxuriant fancy, and even his chairs were covered with 'bibelots' and Tangara statuettes. His scout had to wear slippers – a creak would have caused him agony – and the operation of extraction of a cork from a bottle was performed in his bedroom. The vulgarity of a "pop" was thus obviated…Surely he ought to have been ragged severely for these things, but, though other men were penalised for much less, I never heard of any such visitation on Oscar…In Hall he was a clever talker of the monopolistic type…dining in ordinary clothes was one of his abominations. 'If I were all alone marooned in some desert island and had my things with me, I should dress for dinner every evening'.

Oscar Wilde was a generous and fre-quent host. One of his Oxford friends

LEFT: A sketch of Tom Quad, Christ Church, Oxford, by John Ruskin (1819–1900). Ruskin was Slade Professor of Arts at Oxford whilst Wilde was an undergraduate there. 'The only one [of the great figures in Oxford in the 1870s] who might have influenced Wilde was Ruskin,' thought one of his contemporaries, 'and yet the cult of peacock feathers, sunflowers and velveteen breeches does not suggest Ruskin.'

OSCAR WILDE

remembered that his Sunday evening salon offered 'two brimming bowls of gin-and-whisky punch; and long churchwarden pipes, with a brand of choice tobacco were generally provided for the guests…there was generally music', and when 'the merry guests dispersed', Wilde and his close friends gathered round the fire for good conversation since 'the only possible exercise is talk. It is so exhausting not to talk'. Wilde dominated the gatherings: 'Oscar was always the protagonist in these midnight conversations, pouring out a flood of paradoxes, untenable propositions, quaint comments on men and things, and sometimes…"dropping into poetry", spouting yards of verse, either his own, or that of other poets whom he favoured, and spouting it uncommonly well.'

For although to the Oxford hearties Wilde was a figure of fun, or a source of unease, nevertheless he drew around him a select circle of clever young men who shared his preoccupations. His 'greatest chum' was Richard Reginald Harding, who was known as 'Kitten' after the music hall song 'Beg your parding, Mrs Harding/Is my kitting in your garding?' The group also included William Welsford Ward, who was, like Wilde, reading Greats (two years of classical literature followed by two of ancient history and philosophy) nicknamed, inappropriately 'Bouncer' after a character in a comic novel by Cuthbert Bede [Edward Bradley], *Little Mr Bouncer and his Friend Verdant Green* and David Hunter Blair, a serious-minded Mason who subsequently became a Benedictine monk.

But the two Oxford men who most compelled Wilde's attention were the art critics and writers Walter Pater and John Ruskin. Ruskin was Slade Professor of Fine Arts; Pater a Fellow of Brasenose College. Pater, whose *Studies in the History of the Renaissance*, published in 1873, Wilde pronounced as 'the Holy writ of beauty', was a sensualist: he believed that throughout life man should seek 'not the fruit of experience, but experience itself' – even if that experience might be tinged with the sinister, and certainly with the wanton. Ruskin, however, was a moralist with high Christian social ideals and a taste for nature, particularly as it was found in

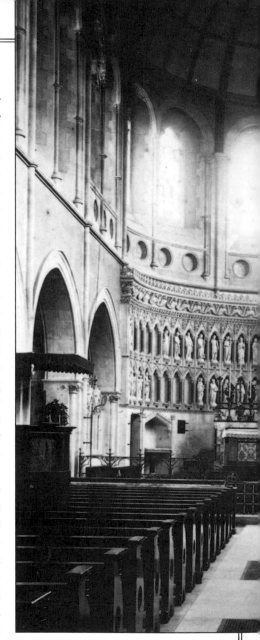

'YOUTH HAS A KINGDOM WAITING FOR IT'

the Swiss mountains, the English lakes and celebrated in the cathedral cities of northern France. His views formed a challenging contrast to the more luxuriant and fleshy pleasure that Pater took in the works of Leonardo da Vinci and Botticelli.

Wilde found Pater's views persuasive and his work was to have 'a strange influence' over his life, but it was in Ruskin that Wilde perceived 'something of prophet, of priest, and of poet, and to you the gods gave eloquence such as they have given to none other, so that your message might come to us with the fire of passion, and the marvel of music, making the deaf to hear and the blind to see.' His commitment to Ruskin was so strong that Oscar was even prepared to take exercise, rising in the early morning to join a gang of undergraduates in building a road across a swampy area in Ferry Hinksey, just outside Oxford. According to a fellow undergraduate, 'Wilde was one of the most regular navvies...specially invited to fill the great man's barrow, and help him trundle it down the plank...as a reward there was a "breakfast" in Ruskin's rooms at Corpus and much talk from him.' Wilde was to extol this aesthete's toil whilst lecturing in America several years later:

> I felt that if there was enough spirit amongst the young men to go out to such
> work as road-making for the sake of a noble ideal of life, I could from them create
> an artistic movement that might change, as it has changed the face of England.

The road, however, was never finished; the face of England remained unchanged. When Ruskin left for a holiday in Venice, the dedicated working party, without his inspiration, lost their application.

Wilde had attended Ruskin's lectures in the Michaelmas Term on 'The Aesthetic and Mathematical School in Florence' and was anxious to visit the city. It was customary at that time for young men with taste and the necessary means to acquire an education to undertake a somewhat scaled-down version of the European Grand Tour, so in the summer vacation of 1875 Wilde went to Italy travelling with his former tutor, Mahaffy, and a

ABOVE. *Oscar Wilde and friends, Oxford, 13 March 1876. Wilde is standing on the right. 'Wilde's bonhomie, good humour, unusual capacity for pleasant talk, and Irish hospitality, exercised much beyond his modest means, soon achieved for him popularity extending far beyond the circle of fellow scholars,' recalled one of his Oxford friends.*

Oscar Wilde

ABOVE: *A photograph showing Oxford students at work on Ruskin's road-building project in Ferry Hinksey. Wilde's admiration for Ruskin made him a willing 'navvy', but the enthusiasm for the work foundered when Ruskin went abroad.*

young Dublin man, William Golding. Writing to his father, Oscar detailed the city's many delights: the 'wonderfully illuminated missals and unreadable manuscripts and autographs' housed in the Biblioteca Laurenziana in the cloisters of San Lorenzo, in which 'I remarked the extreme clearness of the initial letters in the Italian missals and bibles, so different from those in the Book of Kells in the library at Trinity College, Dublin which might stand for anything'.

New sights and experiences were everwhere. In the same letter, Oscar described how he 'dined at a restaurant on top of San Miniato, air delightfully clear and cool after a thunderstorm. Coming back I met just opposite the Pitti Palace, a wonderful funeral; a long procession of monks bearing torches; all in white and wearing a long linen veil over their faces – only their eyes can be seen. They bore two coffins and looked like those awful monks you see in pictures of the Inquisition'.

The party then left Florence *en route* for Milan. Wilde was 'so busy travelling and sight-seeing for the last five days that I have had no time to write'; but on reaching Milan he wrote to tell his mother about his journey in the form of a diary. He had arrived at Venice in early morning of Sunday, 20 June 1875; the approach had reminded him of 'the Bog of Allen, only flatter' and the group were 'seized on immediately by gondoliers and embarked with our luggage, into a *black* hearse-like barge, such as King Arthur was taken away after the fatal battle'. He thrilled to the beauties of Venice, finding 'the Church of San Marco is the most gorgeous; a splendid *Byzantine* church, covered with gilding and mosaics, inside and out'. Wilde

ABOVE: *A sketch by Oscar Wilde of an Etruscan Sarcophagus which he saw on his travels in Rome.*

RIGHT: View from San Miniato, Florence *by John Ruskin, 1875. When Ruskin visited Florence as a young man in 1854, he wrote home 'I begin to feel the effects of the violent excitement of the great art at Florence.' It was in part his lectures on Florentine art and architecture at Oxford that inspired Wilde to see the city on his first visit to Italy in the summer of 1875. He too found it enthralling, and was so busy sight-seeing there that for five days he had 'no time' to describe its attractions to his mother.*

'YOUTH HAS A KINGDOM WAITING FOR IT'

and Mahaffy took a gondola the same afternoon 'and visited some of the islands off Venice; on one an Armenian monastery where Byron used to live…another, the Lido, a favourite place on Sunday', where they had oysters and shrimps before returning to the city 'in the flood of a great sunset. Venice as a city just risen from the sea; a long line of crowded churches and palaces; everywhere white or gilded domes and tall campaniles…a great pink sunset with a long line of purple thunderclouds behind the city.'

Everything that he saw in Venice seemed to conspire to enchant Wilde. A 'wonderful moon' rose as the party returned from the theatre and watching 'a good circus…we landed from our gondola…at the Lion of St Mark. The scene was so romantic that it seemed to be an "artistic" scene from an opera. Believe me,' he insisted in a letter to his mother, 'Venice in beauty of architecture and colour is beyond description. It is the meeting-place of the Byzantine and Italian art – a city belonging to the *East* as much as to the West.'

The next stop, Padua, satisfied Wilde's aesthetic sensibilities less through its architecture 'a quaint town with good colonnades along each street, a university like a barracks, one charming church (Sant' Anastasia) and a lot of bad ones', than by the art which the city housed. The Giotto frescoes so suffused him 'with wonder and reverence and above all love for the scene he has painted' that he felt unable to tell his mother 'of the beauty and purity of sentiment, the clear transparent colour, bright as the day it was painted…[Giotto] is the first of all painters.' From Padua the next halt was at Verona, where they saw an indifferent performance of *Hamlet*, 'but you can imagine how romantic it was to sit in the old amphitheatre (as perfect inside as in the old Roman times) on a lovely moonlight night.' The cathedral at Milan, where the party arrived 'in a shower of rain' was 'an awful failure…Outside the design is monstrous and inartistic. The over-elaborate details stuck high up where no one can see them; everything is vile in it; it is, however, imposing and gigantic as a failure, through its great size and elaborate execution.' However, Wilde's aestheticism was to find a

resonance in the Picture Gallery where, although there were 'some good Correggios and Peruginos, the gem of the whole collection is a lovely Madonna by Bernardino standing among a lot of trellised roses that Morris and Rossetti would love; another by him we saw in the library with a background of lilies.'

From Milan, Mahaffy and Goulding set out for Genoa and thence to Rome, but as he 'had no money', Oscar was 'obliged to leave them and felt very lonely. We have had a delightful tour,' he concluded. The next year Wilde was to write to an Oxford friend, William Ward: 'The extreme beauty of Italy may ruin you, as I think it has done me, for hard work.'

However, it was the eternal city that held a special fascination for Wilde and framed his poem, 'Rome Unvisited':

> And here I set my face towards home,
> For all my pilgrimage is done,
> Although, methinks, yon blood-red sun
> Marshals the way to holy Rome.

RIGHT: A photograph of David Hunter Blair, one of Oscar Wilde's friends. Hunter Blair converted to Roman Catholicism at Oxford; he became a Benedictine monk and then abbot. Blair 'never abandoned' hopes of Wilde's 'ultimate conversion' and supplied 'the wherewithal' for his journey to Rome in 1876 by staking 'a couple of pounds…at Monte Carlo; and if it is predestined that you are to come to Rome, I shall certainly win the money. A rash enterprise'. But Blair's 'star was in the ascendant' and he won £60.

Wilde's friend David Hunter Blair went to Rome at Easter 1875, and was received into the Roman Catholic Church – where he was 'duly blessed by the venerable Pontiff Pius IX'. This was unsettling news for Wilde, who felt very drawn to the Catholic Church himself. His rooms were scattered with photographs of the Pope and Cardinal Manning and he prominently displayed a plaster Madonna. Nevertheless, he feared the wrath of the sternly Protestant Sir William, should he embrace Rome – and he felt drawn to other forms of ritual too.

'I have got rather keen on Masonry lately and believe in it awfully,' he wrote to Ward, 'in fact would be awfully sorry to have to give it up in case I secede from the Protestant Heresy.' Sir William was a Mason in Dublin, and his son had had to get the rules of entry waived in order to become a member of the university's Apollo Lodge before he was twenty-one. A friend and fellow Mason recognized that Wilde was as much struck with

RIGHT: The North-West Angle of the Façade of St Mark's, Venice, *by John Ruskin. Wilde visited the city in June 1875 and was fascinated by the mixture of Eastern and Western artistic influences. He found the 'Church of San Marco…most gorgeous; a splendid* Byzantine *church, covered with gilding and mosaics, inside and out…splendid gates of bronze, everything glorious. Next to it the Doge's Palace, which is beyond praise,' he wrote to his mother.*

the gorgeousness of the Masonic costume, which included knee breeches, tail coat, white tie, silk stockings and pumps, 'as he was amazed at the mystery of our conversation'.

Yet still the compelling lure of Roman Catholicism held Wilde in thrall: 'I now…go to St Aloysius, talk sentimental religion and altogether am caught in the fowler's snare, in the wiles of the Scarlet Woman – I may go over in the vac. I have dreams of a visit to Newman, of the holy sacrament in a new Church, and of a quiet and peace afterwards in my soul. I need not say, though, that I shift with every breath of thought and am weaker and more self-deceiving than ever. If I *could hope* that the Church would wake in me some earnestness and purity I would go over *as a luxury*, if for no better reasons. But I can hardly hope that to go over to Rome would be to sacrifice and give up my two great gods "Money and Ambition".'

Wilde set out for Rome in the spring of 1877. His father had died the previous April, so one restraint to his conversion had been removed. However, one had been added to his freedom of movement, for Sir William's death had revealed the parlous state of the family's finances. It appeared that he had saved nothing and generously endowed the mothers of his illegitimate children.

On this journey, as before, Wilde travelled with Mahaffy and two other young men. Wilde had intended to go only as far as Genoa with them, but, as he wrote somewhat ingenuously to his tutor at Magdalen on 2 April 1877, 'My old tutor Mr Mahaffy, Fellow of Trinity College Dublin, met me on my way to Rome and insisted on my going with him to Mykenae and Athens. The chance of seeing such great places – and in such good company was too great for me and I find myself now in Corfu.' The travellers spent time in Genoa, then visited Ravenna during Holy Week, leaving by the ferry from Brindisi on the night of Easter Sunday. Mahaffy's name opened the doors of Hellas. The director of the German excavations at Olympia showed them round the site, and at Mycenae they were given access to Schliemann's newly excavated treasures. Wilde left Mahaffy and

LEFT: *A portrait of the artist and critic John Ruskin by H. van Herkomer, 1879. 'The dearest memories of my Oxford days are my walks and talks with you, and from you I learned nothing but what was good…there is in you something of prophet, of priest and of poet,' wrote Wilde in May 1888 when he sent Ruskin a copy of his fairy stories* The Happy Prince and Other Tales.

RIGHT: *A photograph of the grave circle at Mycenae in Greece in the 1870s. Schliemann's recent excavations were a great tourist attraction. 'Mahaffy my old tutor carried me off to Greece with him,' wrote Wilde. George Macmillan, son of the publisher, who was also in the party, noted 'Wilde is a very nice fellow whose line lies decidedly in the direction of culture'.*

his companions, sailed to Naples through a violent storm and travelled on to Rome, where the anything but disinterested Hunter Blair had arranged a private audience for him with the Pope. The profundity of spending Easter Day in the Holy City particularly appealed to Wilde; he wrote a poem about it and sent a copy to the then leader of the Liberal opposition, William Ewart Gladstone, who had been encouraging about an earlier poem of Wilde's which applauded his outrage at the Bulgarian massacres:

> *The silver trumpets rang across the dome:*
> *The people knelt upon the ground with awe,*
> *And borne upon the necks of men I saw,*
> *Like some great God, the Holy Lord of Rome.*

But Wilde did not convert to Roman Catholicism; that 'kiss of forgiveness' was to be bestowed upon him only on his deathbed. He wrote later of the religious ambivalence of his fictional character, Dorian Gray:

LEFT: *A statue of a young discus thrower discovered during the excavations at Olympia, Greece. Wilde's fascination with the form of ancient Greek statuary is like Pater's description of Winckelmann in his* Studies in the History of the Renaissance: *his 'affinity with Hellenism was not merely intellectual, that the subtler threads of temperament were interwoven in it, is proved by his romantic, fervid friendships with young men. He has known, he said, many young men more beautiful than Guido's archangel.'*

RIGHT: Head of Lough Corrib, *Connemarra, by John Faulkner. 'We are at the top of Lough Corrib, which if you refer to your geography you will find to be a lake thirty miles long, ten broad and situated in the most romantic scenery in Ireland,' Wilde wrote when he came home to Ireland after he was rusticated from Oxford in 1877.*

It was rumoured of him that he was about to join the Roman Catholic communion; and certainly the Roman ritual had a great attraction for him…But he never fell into the error of arresting his intellectual development by any formal acceptance of a creed or system, or of mistaking, for a house in which to live, an inn that is but suitable for the sojourn of a night in which there are no stars and the moon is in travail…no theory of life seemed to him to be of any importance compared with life itself…

When Wilde returned to Oxford he found that he had been rusticated [temporarily sent down]. It was a month into term before he presented himself at Magdalen after his classical and religious peregrinations; his punishment was a fine and to be 'sent down from Oxford for being the first undergraduate to visit Olympia', as he would later claim.

Wilde's Oxford career so far had been marked with a mixture of indolence, arrogance and brilliance. In March 1876 he wrote to Ward, a fellow Demy, 'I have not done so much reading as I thought I would, but am going to turn over a new leaf this week.' David Hunter Blair was not

entirely convinced by Wilde's academic insouciance: 'he liked to pose as a dilettante trifling with his books; but I knew of the hours of assiduous and laborious reading…Oscar did a great deal of reading surreptitiously in his small and stuffy bedroom, where books lay in apparent hopeless confusion, though he knew where to lay his hands on each in every corner.'

Nevertheless Wilde affected a languid disinterest in the Divinity paper of his second year Honours Moderation exams [Mods], and spoke of the 'Forty-Nine Articles' to the Proctor of the Examination Schools. 'The Thirty-Nine, you mean, Mr Wilde,' corrected the Proctor. Subscribing to the belief that examinations were occasions when 'the foolish ask questions that the wise cannot answer', Wilde failed. The classical paper, however, engaged his interest both in translation and in discussing Aristotle's poetics and, despite an inauspicious start, the oral examination was a triumph. Oscar recounted in a letter to William Ward on 10 July:

> My dear Boy, I know you will be glad to hear I have got a First all right. I came up from Lincolnshire to town on Monday and went down that night to Magdalen to read my Catullus, but while lying in bed on Tuesday morning with Swinburne (a copy of) was woke by the Clerk of the Schools to know why I had not come up. I thought I was not in till Thursday. About one o'clock I nipped up and was ploughed immediately in Divinity and then got a delightful viva voce , first in the Odyssey, where we discussed epic poetry in general, dogs and women, then in Aeschylus where we talked of Shakespeare, Walt Whitman and the Poetics. He had a long discussion about my essay on Poetry in the Aristotle paper and altogether was delightful. Of course I knew I had got a First, so swaggered horribly…My poor mother is in great delight and I was overwhelmed with telegrams on Thursday from everyone I know. My father would have been so pleased about it.

But now what Wilde called the 'boorish insensitivity' of the Magdalen classics tutor and 'the wretched time-serving of that old woman in petticoats, the Dean' had condemned the young scholar to the prospect of

LEFT: *Florence Balcombe, an early love of Wilde's, in his own sketch. 'I am just going out to bring an exquisitely pretty girl to afternoon service in the Cathedral. She is just seventeen with the most perfectly beautiful face I ever saw and not a sixpence of money. I will show you her photograph when I see you next,' wrote Wilde to Reginald Harding in August 1876.*

a Michaelmas term spent in limbo, mainly in Ireland.

Wilde was aware that he had been fortunate in his Mods, and could not count on the same luck in his final examination. He wrote to William Ward in July 'I am going down to Connemara for a month or more next week to try and read. I have not opened a book yet, I have been so bothered with business and other matters. I shall be quite alone. Will you come? I will give you fishing and scenery – and bring your books – *and some notebooks for me*. I am in despair about "Greats".'

LEFT: *Magdalen College, where Wilde read 'Greats' [Classics]. An Oxford friend of those formative years reflected 'It is difficult to trace the Oxford mark on Wilde's after life. He came* blasé, *a Greek scholar, an inveterate talker, and he left much the same except that his talk was cleverer. He certainly influenced Oxford...but no one caught the mantle of his strange personality.'*

But Oscar Wilde's despair was misplaced. On 19 July 1878 it was announced that he had been awarded a First. 'My dear old Boy,' he wrote ecstatically to Ward, 'You are the best of fellows to telegraph your congratulations. It is too delightful altogether this display of fireworks at the end of my career. I cannot understand my First except for the essays which I was fairly good in. I got a very complimentary *viva voce*.

'The dons are "astonied" beyond words – the Bad Boy doing so well in the end! They made me stay up for the Gaudy [the annual college dinner for graduates. It was unusual for an alumni to be invited until he had been 'down' – graduated – for several years] and said nice things about me.'

But the 'Bad Boy' not only had a double first, he had also been awarded the Newdigate Prize for Poetry for his poem on the subject set for that year, 'Ravenna'. The choice of subject was a happy coincidence for Wilde. Exactly a year before the closing date, 31 March 1878, Oscar had entered the city on his way to Greece – though by train, not as he had written:

Newdigate Prize Poem.

—

RAVENNA.

RECITED IN

THE THEATRE, OXFORD,

JUNE 26, 1878.

BY

OSCAR WILDE,

MAGDALEN COLLEGE.

OXFORD:

THOS. SHRIMPTON AND SON, BROAD STREET.

1878.

ABOVE: *The title page of 'Ravenna', the poem that won Wilde the prestigious Newdigate Prize. The subject was fortuitous for Wilde, as 'on 31st of March 1877, long before the subject was announced, I entered Ravenna on my way to Greece, and on 31st March 1878 I had to hand my poem in. It is quite the blue ribbon of the Varsity...'*

I rode at will: the moist glad air was sweet:
The white road rang beneath my horse's feet.

Speranza was ecstatic. 'Oh Gloria, Gloria!' she wrote:

…thank you a million times for the telegram. It is the first throb of joy I have had this year. How I long to read the poem. Well, after all, we have Genius …This gives you a certainty of success in the future – You can now trust your own intellect, and know what it can do. I should so like to see the smile on your face now. Ever and ever with joy and pride.
Your loving Mother.

But how was the Genius to live? The college did not translate its 'astonishment' into the offer of a Fellowship. His friend William Ward forced Oscar to confront the unwelcome prospect of his unresolved future. He was later to remember Wilde's vigorous response:

'You talk a lot about yourself, Oscar,' said Ward. 'and all the things you would like to achieve. But you never say what you are going to do with your life. Dunsky [Hunter Blair] here is destined to be a Scottish laird – probably in a kilt; and I shall settle down as a blameless lawyer at Bristol, and keep the three degrees of comparison steadily in view. But you, Oscar, who have twice as much brains in that ridiculous head of yours as both of us put together – what are you going to *do* with them? What is your real ambition in life?' 'God knows,' said Oscar, serious for a moment. 'I won't be a dried-up Oxford don, anyhow. I'll be a poet, a writer, a dramatist. Somehow or other I'll be famous, and if not famous, I'll be notorious.'

ABOVE: *A sketch by Wilde from a manuscript page of his poem 'The Sphinx' It shows two schoolmasters chasing some pupils. Yet Wilde periodically thought about education as a possible career option after Oxford. In 1880 he asked Oscar Browning, a Cambridge don, for a 'testimonial for a position in the Education Office or School Inspectorship …Rents being as extinct in Ireland as the dodo or moly, I want to get a position with an assured income, and any Education work would be very congenial to me.'*

CHAPTER 2

'IT IS ALWAYS NICE TO BE EXPECTED
AND NOT TO ARRIVE'

'I remember when I was at Oxford,' Wilde wrote in *De Profundis*, 'saying to one of my friends…that I wanted to eat the fruit of all the trees in the garden of the world, and that I was going out into the world with that passion in my soul. And so indeed, I went out, and so lived.' In 1878 Oscar Wilde left Oxford and Dublin for London.

In doing so, he also left his first love. He had met Florence Balcombe, the daughter of an Army officer, in August 1876 when he was twenty-one and she seventeen. Oscar thought Florence – possibly named after Florence Nightingale, whom her father had met whilst he was serving in the Crimea – 'exquisitely pretty'; in a poem he admired her '… delicate / Fair body made for love and pain', and he gave her a small gold cross with their names inscribed on it. But Wilde was a student with no money. Florence had no dowry. He may have found her enchanting, and sent her a watercolour he had painted, but equally he flirted with other Dublin girls, and had reported finding the left leg of a young Greek boy 'a poem'. In 1877 he found the portrait of a young boy so exquisite that he penned a sonnet:

> *A fair slim boy not made for this world's pain,*
> *With hair of gold thick clustering round his ears…*
> *Pale cheeks whereon no kiss hath left its stain,*
> *Red under-lip drawn in for fear of Love,*
> *And white throat whiter than the breast of dove –*

This was published in *Kottabos*, the classics magazine of Trinity College, Dublin, edited by his former tutor, Tyrrell. When it was republished in a volume of Wilde's collected poems in 1881 the 'fair slim boy…With hair

LEFT: *Wilde was prominently featured as a critic in W.P. Frith's* A Private View at the Royal Academy, *painted in 1881. Lillie Langtry, Frederic Leighton, Henry Irving, the Archbishop of York, Millais and a lady wearing the inevitable sunflower are all represented in the crush around Wilde, listening to the pronouncements of the critic. Wilde was not an admirer of the 'realism' of Victorian genre paintings. He once reviewed 'Mr Frith' as someone 'who has done so much to elevate painting to the dignity of photography'.*

of gold thick clustering round his ears' had become 'A lily-girl' who was 'not made for this world's pain' either, but was endowed with 'brown, soft hair close braided by her ears'. The poem, formerly inscribed 'Wasted Days', was now titled 'Madonna Mia'. Beauty, like sexuality, was still negotiable and mutable.

But there were new delights in the metropolis. 'I often have beautiful people to tea, and will always be very glad to see you and introduce you to them,' Wilde wrote to a former Oxford friend on 23 December 1879. 'Any night you like to go to the theatre I will give you a bed with great pleasure in this untidy and romantic house.' Wilde's acquaintance with London high society was greatly helped by sharing lodgings at Thames House, off the Strand, with an old friend – affable, unstable Frank Miles, who found that his modest artistic talent gave him an *entrée* into high society.

Lillie Langtry was avowedly the most beautiful of the very beautiful people with whom Miles and that proselytizer for beauty, Oscar Wilde, contrived to surround themselves. She was the most sought-after beauty in London and eventually became the mistress of Edward, Prince of Wales. And the Thames House men used their particular talents in oblation: Miles to sketch this Venus; Wilde to shower his icon with lilies, take her to lectures on the classics, tutor her in Latin and write poems to her. Styling her 'The New Helen' [of Troy], his hyperbole flew:

LEFT: *An etching of St James's Street, London, by James McNeill Whistler, a frequent visitor at Thames House where Wilde and Frank Miles shared rooms. Whistler wrote 'I am bored to death after a certain time away from Piccadilly.' Wilde praised his fellow metropolitan* flâneur *as the 'first painter in England, only it will take England 300 years to find it out'.*

> *Lily of love, pure and inviolate!*
> *Tower of ivory! red rose of fire!*
> *Thou hast come down our darkness to illume:*
> *And the white glory of thy loveliness.*

It was not Wilde's looks that captured Mrs Langtry. She described him as appearing 'so colourless that a few pale freckles of good size were oddly conspicuous. He had a well shaped mouth, with somewhat coarse lips and greenish-hued teeth. The plainness of his face, however, was redeemed by the splendour of his great, eager eyes'. She noted his 'large and indolent hands' with 'perfect shaped [if not very clean] filbert nails' and 'one of the most alluring voices that I have ever listened to, round and soft, and full of variety and expression'. A letter written to Wilde in 1879, gives a shrewd indication of the nature of their attraction for each other:

> Of course I'm longing to learn more Latin but...I shan't be able to see my kind tutor before Thursday. Do come and see me on that afternoon about six if you can. I called at Salisbury Street about an hour before you left. I wanted to ask you how I should go to a fancy ball here, but I chose a soft black Greek dress with a fringe of silver crescents and stars, and diamond ones in my hair and on my neck, and called it Queen of [the] Night. I made it myself.

As both launched their particular form of genius on the London scene, each needed a friend to practise – and rely – upon.

Oscar Wilde was clearly making an impression as an aesthete who pronounced with an erudite and pithy wit, a stylish *bon viveur*, an amusing and sought-after host and guest, a spectacle. The floor he occupied at Thames House was entirely panelled in white, decorated with Greek rugs and hangings, tiles from Damascus, drawings by Blake and Burne Jones, and ornamented with his Tanagra figures, blue china and swathes of lilies. His clothes were carefully thought out – 'quite the dog', and when a man was overheard at the theatre to remark: 'there goes that bloody fool Oscar Wilde', 'the fool' was not displeased: 'It's extraordinary how soon one gets known in London,' he remarked. In 1881 the Prince of Wales himself sought to meet Wilde – which he did at a séance at the Wilde/Miles *ménage* – saying 'I do not know Mr Wilde, and not to know Mr Wilde is not to be known.' But 'getting known' hardly represented either a career or the full realization of genius – nor did it provide an income. For Wilde, social success could be only a beginning.

The burgeoning aesthetic movement – or 'craze', as its detractors called it – had become familiar to London society. If not understood, it could be easily caricatured, and Wilde was its natural exemplar.

LEFT: *The actress Lillie Langtry, 'the adored and adorable Lily', as Wilde called her, photographed by Van der Weyde in New York. The year before his death he confided to a journalist that 'the three women I have most admired are Queen Victoria, Sarah Bernhardt and Lillie Langtry. I would have married any one of them with pleasure'.*

OSCAR WILDE

The cartoonist (and later novelist and author of *Trilby*), George du Maurier, introduced the readers of *Punch* to two 'aesthetic types' – the poet Jellaby Postlethwaite and the painter, Maudle. He included in their antics a character with flowing locks and a predilection for blue china called variously Oscuro Wildgoose, Drawit Wilde, the Wilde-eyed poet and Ossian Wilderness. In the spring of 1881 the mockery reached its apotheosis in the comic opera *Patience*. This was the work of the collaborators Gilbert, the versifier, and the composer Sullivan, who had achieved their first joint success with *Trial by Jury* in 1875.

Patience opened on 23 April 1881. It was an immediate success and was to play for a year in London before touring the provinces. The main characters were poets. Reginald Bunthorne was a 'fleshly poet' while Archibald Grosvenor was an 'idyllic poet' and whilst both were an amalgam of the aesthetes – including Swinburne, Ruskin and Rossetti – each also drew

ABOVE: *A portrait of Ellen Terry, another actress whom Wilde hoped would perform in his plays. He wrote a poem to her following her performance as Henrietta Maria, wife of Charles I:.*

'She stands with eyes marred by the
mists of pain
Like some wan lily overdrenched with
rain…
O Hair of Gold! O Crimson Lips! O
Face
Made for the lurings and the love of
man!'

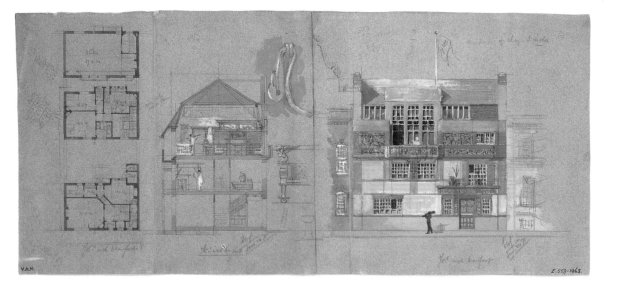

reference directly from Wilde. The actor George Grossmith played Bunthorne with the painter Whistler's mannerisms and appurtenances, though he spoke lines that parodied Oscar, 'It is the wail of the poet's heart on discovering that everything is commonplace. To understand it, cling passionately to one another and think of faint lilies'. He also sang the highly popular ditty:

Though the Philistines may jostle, you may rank as an
apostle in the high aesthetic band,
If you walk down Piccadilly with a poppy
or a lily in your medieval hand.

LEFT: *Sheet music for the* Patience Quadrille, *following the success of the Gilbert and Sullivan opera* Patience. *It was claimed that this satire on the aesthetic movement sought not ' to cast ridicule on the true aesthetic spirit, but only to attack the unmanly oddities which masquerade in its likeness.'*

Not that Wilde ever had. But that, as he himself acknowledged, was not the point: 'To have done it was nothing,' he scoffed, 'but to make people think one had done it was a triumph.'

Speranza and Willie had moved to London, too, where Oscar's brother was trying without conspicuous success to make a living as a journalist. Lady Wilde was struggling to make ends meet and finance her weekly literary and society salon by editing her late husband's work and putting together collections of her own memoirs, essays and verse.

Oscar was writing too. He was now set on becoming a playwright. It was a natural progression. Wilde's talent was the spoken word, conversation – or monologue – the preferred vehicle for his ideas, and actresses were his natural companions. Apart from Lillie Langtry's nascent theatrical ambitions, Wilde had made the acquaintance of the greatest actress of the nineteenth century, Sarah Bernhardt, who had arrived in England in May 1879 to star in Racine's *Phèdre*. Wilde took himself to Folkestone to meet her boat and pay her homage in his usual currency – lilies. At the first night of *Phèdre* he conceived the conceit – which he was to pursue later with some doggedness – of having Bernhardt appear in a play that he had written, or rather would one day write. In the meantime he dedicated his poem *Phèdre*, cast in the classic mould, to her:

OSCAR WILDE

…Ah! surely once some urn of Attic clay
Held thy wan dust, and thou hast come again
Back to this common world so dull and vain,
For thou wert weary of the sunless day,
The heavy fields of scentless asphodel,
The loveless lips with which men kiss in Hell.

Ellen Terry, whom Wilde saw in June 1879 in the play *Charles I* by his relation W. G. Wills, received similar treatment. In September he unsuccessfully sent Miss Terry a specially bound copy of a play he had written entitled *Vera: or The Nihilists*, dedicated with the hope that 'Perhaps some day I shall be fortunate to write something worthy of your playing'. The play was based on the assassination of the governor of St Petersburg by a young woman, Vera Zassoulich, a Nihilist, in 1878 – an act which reverberated throughout the world.

However, despite these attempts to achieve recognition as a playwright, Wilde was still primarily a poet. He had written poetry since his days at Trinity College, Dublin, and had some thirty poems already published in magazines. In April 1881, he approached a publisher:

> Dear Sir, I am anxious to publish a volume of poems immediately, and should like to enter into a treaty with your house about it. I can forward you the manuscript on hearing that you will begin negotiations. Possibly my name needs no introduction. Yours truly, Oscar Wilde.

At Wilde's expense, 750 copies were printed on hand-made paper with fine parchment binding. The first poem was 'Hélas', which could have been read both as a questioning apologia and as a powerful prefiguration:

> *To drift with every passion till my soul*
> *Is a stringed lute upon which all winds can play,*
> *Is it for this that I have given away*
> *Mine ancient wisdom and austere control?*

DRAWN BY GEORGE DU MAURIER.

MAUDLE ON THE CHOICE OF A PROFESSION.

Maudle. "How consummately lovely your Son is, Mrs. Brown!"

Mrs. Brown (a Philistine from the country). "What! He's a nice manly Boy, if you mean that, Mr. Maudle. He has just left School, you know, and wishes to be an Artist."

Maudle. "Why should he *Be* an Artist!"

Mrs. Brown. "Well, he must be *something*!"

Maudle. "Why should he *Be* anything! Why not let him remain for ever content *to* Exist *Beautifully*!"

[Mrs. Brown determines that at all events her Son shall not study Art under Maudle.

MAUDLE ON THE CHOICE OF A PROFESSION. 1881.

AN ÆSTHETIC MIDDAY MEAL.

[At the Luncheon hour Jellaby Postlethwaite enters a Pastrycook's and calls for a glass of Water, into which he puts a freshly-cut Lily, and loses himself in contemplation thereof.

Waiter. "Shall I bring you anything else, Sir?"

Jellaby Postlethwaite. "Thanks, no! I have all I require, and shall soon have done!"

AN ÆSTHETIC MIDDAY MEAL. 1880.

'IT IS ALWAYS NICE TO BE EXPECTED...'

RIGHT: *A photograph of Oscar Wilde by Napoleon Sarony, taken in New York in 1882. In his early London days, Wilde had become a target for satire, but his achievements after Oxford were still few. 'What has he done, this young man that one meets everywhere? Oh yes, he talks well, but what has he done? He has written nothing, he does not sing, or paint, or act – he does nothing but talk.' The Polish actress, Helena Modjeska, articulated what many were thinking when she arrived in London in 1880.*

Matthew Arnold, to whom Wilde had sent a copy, praised his 'true feeling for rhythm...which is at the bottom of all success in poetry'. Others were not so kind. *Punch* called it 'Swinburne and water' and suggested:

> The poet is Wilde
> But his poetry's tame.

The sharpest laceration came from his own university. The secretary of the Oxford Union requested a copy; Wilde obliged. Oliver Elton, later a historian of English literature, vehemently objected to the acquisition:

> It is not that the poems are thin – and they are thin: it is not that they are immoral – and they are immoral: it is not that they are this or that – and they are all this and that: it is that they are for the most part not by their putative father at all, but by a number of better known and deservedly reputed authors. They are in fact by William Shakespeare, by Philip Sidney, by John Donne, by Lord Byron, by William Morris, by Algernon Swinburne, and by sixty more, whose works have furnished the list of passages which I hold in my hand at this moment.

The members of the Union voted by a narrow margin against accepting the book with its modest shelf space requirement and the librarian reluctantly returned the requested copy. Wilde responded with dignity, regretting that 'there should still be at Oxford such a large number of young men who are ready to accept their own ignorance as an index, and their own conceit as a criterion of any imaginative and beautiful work.'

That year and the next, he was to have more evidence of the moral censure, hypocrisy and betrayal that was to be a recurrent *motif* of his life. Given notice to leave Thames House by the filially obsequious Miles, whose clergyman father saw nothing but evil in the *Poems*, Wilde was living in furnished rooms. His meagre income was dwindling alarmingly when a cablegram arrived from New York in September 1881: 'Responsible agent asks me to enquire if you will consider offer he makes for fifty readings, beginning November first'. Here was an opportunity to make money, promote his ideas to an entirely new audience, and leave for a time the narrowing confines of his adopted land. He seized upon it.

Going to America might make Wilde famous: the reason for the invitation was that he was already mildly notorious. The aesthetic movement had proved itself to be 'box office' in England, if only in caricature, and Wilde was aestheticism personified.

Patience had opened in New York in September 1881. A certain Colonel Morse who had organized the tour for the producer of *Patience*, Richard D'Oyly Carte, explained their reasons for inviting Wilde:

> My attention was first drawn to [Wilde] for the reason, that while we were preparing for the opera "Patience" in New York, his name was often quoted as the originator of the aesthetic idea, and the author of a number of poems lately published, which had made a profound sensation in English society. It was suggested to me, that if Mr Wilde were brought to this country with the view of illustrating in a public way his idea of the aesthetic, that not only would society be glad to hear the man and receive him socially, but also that the general public would be interested in hearing from him a true and correct definition and explanation of this latest form of fashionable madness…

Morse offered a choice of three lecture topics which Wilde 'advises me he has prepared…one of which is devoted to a consideration of 'The Beautiful' as seen in everyday life, another, illustrative of the poetical methods used by Shakespeare, and the third, a Lyric Poem.' It was, however, not Wilde the scholar nor Wilde the poet that was going to be the draw in America: it was Wilde the aesthete. 'The Beautiful' was to be his subject.

He also now had an additional reason for wishing to go to America. Just as *Vera* was about to go into rehearsal in London at the end of November 1881, the play was cancelled. Although its subject, according to its author, was 'passion not politics', the assassination of Tsar Alexander II in March had made the subject of republican violence politically sensitive

ABOVE: *A sketch of Wilde at an 'aesthetic reception' from a newspaper of 21 January, 1882. 'I bow graciously and sometimes honour them with a royal observation… Loving virtuous obscurity as I do, you can judge how much I dislike this lionizing…'*

RIGHT: *An aerial view of Philadelphia where Wilde lectured on 17 January 1882. On his arrival 'Mr Wilde…listened with wide-open eyes to an explanation of a long train of oil cars, but did not say if he found any beauty in them…As his conspicuous figure walked through the [railway station] waiting room, many a whispered comment flew about; but the Aesthete dived into a cab and was whirled quickly away to his quarters.'*

ABOVE: *Max Beerbohm's later impression of Wilde's American lectures. 'In America,' explained Wilde, 'I have been face to face with people who have never seen good art… many come to hear me just from curiosity… The great thing is to get them to come.'*

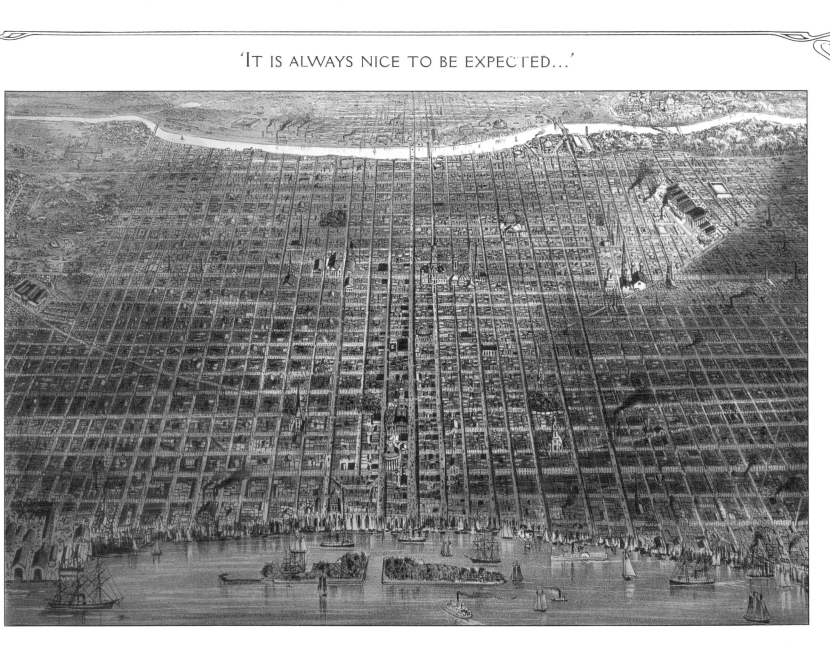

– particularly as the new Tsarina was the sister-in-law of the Prince of Wales. However, the assassination of President Garfield, who died in September 1881, would presumably not have inclined the American authorities either to look favourably on the portrayal of an act of political violence on stage.

Nevertheless, with a degree of naïvety, motives that were mixed and expectations that were to be both confirmed and confounded, Oscar Wilde set sail for America on 24 December 1881.

The *Arizona* docked in New York harbour on the evening of 2 January 1882 and a small posse of press men took a 'row-boat' out to the ship at anchor off Staten Island. A journalist from the *New York Tribune* reported:

> The most striking thing about the poet's appearance is his height, which is several inches over six feet, and the next thing to attract attention is his hair, which is of dark brown colour, and falls down upon his shoulders…When he laughs his lips part widely and show a shining row of upper teeth, which are superlatively white.

The man from the *New York World* pointed out, perhaps with a touch of disappointment, that this disproved 'a pleasing story which has gone the rounds of the English press that he has three tusks or protruberants far from agreeable to look at…' He went on at some length:

> The complexion, instead of being the rosy hue so common in Englishmen, is so utterly devoid of colour that it can only be said to resemble putty…Instead of having a small delicate hand, only fit to caress a lily, his fingers are long and when doubled up would form a fist that would hit a hard knock, should an occasion arise for the owner to descend to that kind of argument…His manner of talking is somewhat affected – judging from the American standpoint – his great peculiarity being a rhythmic chant in which every fourth syllable is accentuated. Thus, when asked what was his mission in America, he replied in a sing-song tone: I came from Eng-land because I thought America was the best place to see.

LEFT: *Punch's view of Wilde's American tour, 11 March 1882, entitled 'Ossian (with Variations) the Son of Ia-Cultcha: Is This the Son of Cultcha's Shadowy Form?' Wilde's view of his tour, expressed a month earlier, did not exactly discourage mockery: 'I have had a sort of triumphal progress, live like a young sybarite, travel like a young god. I am deluged with poems and flowers at every town.'*

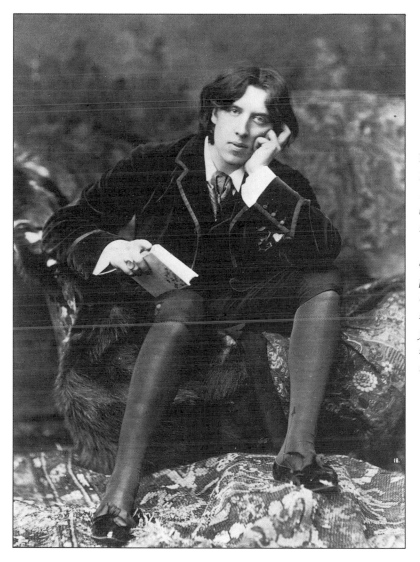

LEFT: *Oscar Wilde, photographed in New York by Napoleon Sarony in January 1882. Anna, Comtesse de Brémont, met the 'apostle of aesthetics' at a dinner party in New York that autumn. She had been 'at a loss to decide whether I was amused or edified by the spectacle of that splendid personage clad in black velvet coat and knee breeches, black silk stockings, low shoes with glittering buckles', but many years later fancied that she had 'read his secret. I saw his feminine soul...revealed in the mirror of those strange eyes...'*

OSCAR WILDE

STRAITON
AND
STORM'S
NEW CIGARS.

AESTHETIC
SUN-FLOWER
TOO TOO
CAPADURA PATIENCE

DEALERS SUPPLIED BY
R.C. BROWN & CO.
NEW YORK.

'OSCAR WILDE.'

ABOVE: *A detail of Wilde lecturing, from an American trade card of the period. Wilde defended the celebrated aesthetic admiration for the sunflower and lily on artistic grounds, 'not for any vegetable fashion at all [but] because these two lovely flowers are…the most perfect models of design, the most naturally adapted for the decorative art…'*

Wilde had prepared himself as an aesthete, and he arrived in the New World wearing 'a befrogged and wonderfully befurred green overcoat' – trimmed with seal or otter, a garment to which he was loyal for many years. On his head he wore a small cap of the same fur and his shirts had a wide Byronic collar, filled in with a sky-blue necktie. His dainty feet were shod in patent leather. The press plied him with questions: 'I have come', said one reporter portentously, 'to ask you as to your intention in visiting this country. And, while we are about it, will you give me your definition of aestheticism?'

'Well,' replied Wilde, 'aestheticism is a search after the signs of the beautiful. It is the science of the beautiful through which men seek the correlation of the arts. It is, to speak more exactly, the search after the secret of life.' And soon after that perplexing reply 'suggesting that there would be much to be made clear in his forthcoming lectures', he disembarked. Sweeping ashore with the possibly apocryphal response to a customs officer 'I have nothing to declare but my genius', Wilde made for Manhattan and was swept up in a frenzy of social engagements, and enthusiasm. He wrote back to England: '…policemen wait for me to clear a way. I now understand why the Royal Boy [the Prince of Wales] is in good humour always: it is delightful to be a *petit roi*. However if I am not a success on Monday [when he was due to give his first lecture] I shall be very wretched.'

He made his debut on 9 January at Chickering Hall, New York, wearing the knee breeches and stockings of his Masonic Lodge. Wilde reported home on the first lecture's success:

> The hall had an audience larger and more wonderful than even Dickens had. I was recalled and applauded and am now treated like the Royal Boy. I have several secretaries. One writes my autograph all day for my admirers, the other receives the flowers that are left really every ten minutes. A third whose hair resembles mine is obliged to send off locks of his own hair to the myriad maidens of the city, and so is rapidly becoming bald.

RIGHT: New York Street Scene *by Hippolyte V. Sebron. 'Oscar Wilde is here,' wrote one Colonel Forbes, who was discoursing on 'The Inner Life of a War Correspondent' on much the same lecture circuit as Wilde was defining the aesthetic. 'He wears knee breeches, but alas no lily…He can't lecture worth a cent, but draws the crowds wonderfully and he fools them all…' Forbes' jealousy at his rival's success led him to put around the story that Wilde had been offered £200 by P.T. Barnum to carry a lily in one hand and a sunflower in the other as he led an elephant through the streets of New York.*

And he rejoiced in another letter:

> I am torn to bits by society. Immense receptions, wonderful dinners, crowds wait for my carriage. I wave a gloved hand and an ivory cane and they cheer. Girls very lovely, men simple and intellectual. Rooms are hung with white lilies for me everywhere. I have 'Boy' [champagne] at intervals…I give sittings to artists, and generally behave as I always have behaved – '*dreadfully*'.

It was a punishing schedule: in the nine months Oscar Wilde spent lecturing in North America from January to October 1882 he zigzagged from the Eastern seaboard to the West Coast, from the Prairies to the Rockies, to Canada and back, in a hectic schedule taking in anywhere in America where an audience could be raised.

There were also some more personal literary visits to organize. 'I do so hope to meet Mr Whitman,' said Wilde. 'Perhaps he is not widely read in England, but England never appreciates a poet until he is dead. There is

BELOW (*left and right*): *A photograph and a sketch of the Colorado town of Leadsville, visited by Wilde in 1882. In a letter to Helena Sickert, he describes 'the great mining city of the west called Leadville [where he] lectured the miners on the old workers in metal – Cellini and others…they were a most courteous audience: typical too – large blonde-bearded, yellow-haired men in red shirts, with beautiful clear complexions of people who work in silver mines.'*

LEFT: *'Something to live up to': a cartoon by Thomas Nast in* Harper's Bazaar *on 10 June 1882, inspired by Wilde's accolade that the Colorado miners were the 'only well-dressed men I have seen in America'. The admiration was mutual, the miners pronouncing Wilde as 'a bully boy with no glass eye'. Wilde responded to this 'artless and spontaneous praise which touched me more than the pompous panegyrics of literary critics ever could or did'.*

THE JUDGE

A THING OF BEAUTY NOT A JOY FOREVER.
Rise and Fall of a "Vera" Wilde Æsthete.

LEFT: *'A Thing of Beauty not a Joy Forever': a caricature of Oscar Wilde's American tour, 1883. One of Oscar Wilde's purposes in going to America was to have* Vera, *his 'new and original drama on Russia', staged in New York. As he explained: 'The note through which the passion of the play is expressed is democratic – and for that reason it's unthinkable to act it in London. It is yet the tragedy, the essence of the play is human.' But it was not to be. In the 1880s Wilde might flourish as an aesthete and a spectacle in America, but as a playwright he was still unsuccessful.*

something so Greek and sane about his poetry, it is so universal, so comprehensive.' Introduced to Whitman's work by Speranza, Wilde held him to be one of the finest American poets. The meeting was arranged and the Philadelphia Press reported Whitman's account of the visit:

I took [Mr Wilde] up to my den…where we had a jolly good time. I think he was glad to get away from lecturing, and fashionable society, and spend time with an 'old rough'…I think him genuine, honest, and manly. I was glad to have him with me, for his youthful health, enthusiasm, and buoyancy are refreshing. He was in his best mood, and I imagine that he laid aside any affectation that he is said to have, and that I saw behind the scenes. He talked freely about the London *literati*…One of the first things I said was that I should call him 'Oscar'. 'I like that so much,' he answered, laying his hand on my knee. He seemed to me like a great big, splendid boy…He's so frank, outspoken and manly. I don't see why such mocking things are written of him.

LEFT: *A photograph of San Francisco, c.1890. 'Do you like our country, Mr Wilde?' quizzed a reporter from the* Daily Examiner San Francisco. *'There is very much here to like and admire,' replied Wilde, who on this occasion 'was dressed in a style that would attract attention anywhere outside an artist's studio… there was no need for anyone to point in order to identify him'.*

The meeting between the two writers was a success. Wilde and the author of *Leaves of Grass* 'talked for two hours' about aspects of literature and art before Whitman made him 'a big glass of milk punch, and he tossed it off and away he went'.

Wilde was 'very silent, and seemed deeply affected by the interview'. His comment some ten years later that 'the kiss of Walt Whitman is still on my lips' was not reported. Whitman, like Wilde, was often to be marginalized by a public disconcerted by his openness about sexual matters.

Oscar Wilde's next encounter with a great American man of letters was to be less satisfactory. He met the novelist Henry James in Washington. James called on Wilde at his hotel, but when the American expressed his nostalgia for London, Wilde was dismissive: 'You care for places? The world is my home'. It was an aphorism that enraged the cultivated, cosmopolitan James. Wilde apparently was unaware of the offence he had caused, and nothing that passed between them caused him to revise his high opinion of James as a novelist. James, however, ranted that 'Hosscar' was 'a fatuous fool, a tenth-rate cad'.

Wherever he went, Wilde was interviewed by the press and answered their questions on art, aesthetics, his views on America and the recurrent subject of his attire: 'the essence of good dressing is perfect congruity. One must be careful not to be too premature, but I feel that at present velvet is the most beautiful dress for a man. As a rule I wear gray or brown velvet myself.' He requested that copies of the papers in which the interviews appeared were sent back to privileged recipients in England: '*three* copies of today's *Press* and three of today's *Times* to Lady Wilde'.

LEFT: *Undergraduates at Harvard, Massachusetts, c.1890. On 31 January 1882 rows of Harvard students turned up for Wilde's lecture clad in knee breeches and clutching a sunflower apiece. 'Save me from my disciples,' sighed Wilde as he surveyed the rows, forewarned and himself wearing conventional evening dress. 'There is more to the movement of aestheticism than knee breeches and sunflowers,' he cautioned the 'caricatures'.*

RIGHT: *A photograph of Broadway in New York, 1887. Wilde's first American lecture took place at Chickering Hall in New York; he delivered a second at Wallack's Theatre on 11 May 1882. The subject was 'Decorative Art' and he informed his audience: 'I would have a workshop attached to every school, and one hour a day given up to the teaching of simple decorative arts. It would be a golden hour to the children. And soon you would raise up a race of handicraftsmen who would transform the face of your country.'*

ABOVE: *A sketch by Wilde of an advertisment for one of his lectures which he could see from the window of his hotel in Montreal in 1882. 'I am now six feet high (my name on the placards), printed it is true in those primary colours against which I pass my life protesting, but still it is fame...I feel I have not lived in vain.'*

RIGHT: *'The Aesthetic versus the Material', a caricature of Oscar Wilde showing what the aesthete really did 'sit up with all night'. The cartoon appeared in* Frank Leslie's Illustrated Newspaper *on 21 January 1882. It seems to have inspired a versifier, Orth Stein:*

Long and thin is the form within
 That rests in the easy chair,
And he counts his pelf,
while high on a shelf
 Is a wig of flowing hair…
Softly, says he, 'what fools they be,
 In this semi-civilized land.
They think that I live on sunflower seed –
 An Irish Stew is more what I need'.

RIGHT: *The cover of Wilde's privately published play,* Vera. *'Write to me what you think of* Vera,' *begged Wilde of the American actress, Mary Anderson, from New York in October 1882.* 'Vera *charms me,' she replied, 'It is very mournful. I think I would like to play the part.' But she finally refused, and the play was to have only the briefest of runs in New York in August 1883.*

When he had first arrived in New York, Wilde had made clear his intentions in coming to lecture in America:

> I should be very disappointed if when I left for Europe I had not influenced in however slight a way the growing spirit of art in this country, very disappointed if I had not out of the many who listen to me made one person love beautiful things a little more, and very disappointed if in return for the dreadfully hard work, of lecturing – hard to me who am inexperienced – I did not earn enough money to give myself an autumn at Venice, a winter at Rome, and a spring at Athens; but all these things are perhaps a dream.

Criss-crossing North America, Wilde took care to set an aesthetic example himself. Writing to Colonel Morse from Missouri at the end of February

1882, he instructed him to 'go to a good costumier (theatrical) for me and get them to make (you will not mention my name) two coats, to wear at matinées and perhaps in the evening. They should be beautiful; tight velvet doublets, with large flowered sleeves and little ruffs of cambric coming up from under the collar. I send you designs and measurements…any good costumier would know what I want – sort of Francis I dress: only knee-breeches instead of long hose…They were dreadfuly disappointed at Cincinnati at my not wearing knee-breeches.'

The American press by no means always treated him kindly. Wilde ostensibly dismissed the mockery, and sometimes hostility, from the newspapers – he was dubbed 'a penny Ruskin' by the *New York Tribune*. In a letter to his solicitor friend George Lewis he commented, 'They talk about yellow fever but I think that one who has survived the press is impregnable', and remarked to a Californian journalist 'There is no limit to the nonsense some men will write if it raises the circulation of the paper from one to two…'

But on the whole Wilde presented the trip in a favourable light. He wrote to Helena Sickert (whom he addressed as 'Miss Nellie') from Salt Lake City, Utah:

> I feel I am doing really good work here, and of course artists have received
> me with enthusiasm everywhere. The excitement I cause would amuse you
> and it amuses me, but the country is full of wonders – buffaloes, Indians, elks
> and the like. It all interests me very much.

And to Norman Forbes-Robertson, the English actor and playwright, he happily boasted:

> I am now six feet high (my name on the placards), printed it is true in those
> primary colours against which I pass my life protesting, but even still it is
> fame, and anything is better than virtuous obscurity, even one's own name in
> alternate colours of Albert blue and magenta six feet tall.

VERA;

OR, THE NIHILISTS.

A Drama

IN A PROLOGUE AND FOUR ACTS.

BY

OSCAR WILDE.

1882.

BELOW: *A photograph of the American actress Marie Prescott, who played Vera during the play's few New York performances.*

He had made some money from his lecture tour, and regarded his mission to civilize America by the moral inspiration of beauty as largely successful. He had extended his repertoire by adding two other lectures: 'The House Beautiful' and 'The Decorative Arts' which gave practical tips for the aesthetic life. The entrance hall of homes should be papered rather than painted, tiled rather than carpeted. Sharing his mother's dislike of too much light, Oscar prescribed small windows and soft wall lights in preference to overhead lighting. He abhorred artificial flowers and advised women to abandon their corsets and settle for a draped, classical Greek look in dress.

Wilde was optimistic about both the immediate achievements of his tour and the effect he hoped it would have upon future aesthetic development:

> Of course I have much to bear – I have always had that – but still as regards my practical influence I have succeeded beyond my wildest hope. In every city they start schools of decorative art after my visit, and set on foot public museums, getting my advice about the choice of objects and the nature of the building.

The Comtesse de Brémont, who met Wilde in New York at the end of his lecture circuit, was to reflect several years later:

> The impression which Oscar Wilde made on the taste of America in the matter of home decoration, was a lasting one. To-day, the horse-hair covered furniture, the ugly wall-paper and coarse stone-ware china, the decorative fly-papers, the glaringly defective house architecture with its ungainly lines and grotesque angles has disappeared. The useful is combined with the beautiful. Every home is a picture in itself. This is what Oscar Wilde did for the great mass of the people – the artisans, the mechanics and even the labourers. His propaganda of art was not lost, for his very eccentricities, his abuse and ridicule by the Press spread the gospel among the people.

The impact of Wilde's lecture tour upon his own situation appeared dramatic. There was no chance any more – if there had ever been – of

ABOVE: *A cartoon of Wilde by 'Ape' (Carlo Pellegrini), one of the 'Men of the day' series published in* Vanity Fair, *1884. It mocked Wilde's 'Nero' curls which marked the advent of his 'second period'. He had modelled his new coiffeur on a bust of the Roman Emperor in the Louvre. 'One should always either be a work of art, or wear a work of art.'*

ABOVE: *A portrait of Edmond de Goncourt by Felix Braquemond. Wilde first met the French novelist, historian, boulevadier and diarist in April 1883. Wilde sent Goncourt a copy of his 'first poetic flowers' as 'a testimony' of his 'infinite admiration for the author of* Le Faustin*'. For his part, Goncourt noted in his* Journal *that Wilde was 'an individual of doubtful sex ['au sexe douteux'], with …barnstormer's language and…tall stories'.*

'virtuous obscurity'. It was obvious that Wilde was as popular a spectacle in England as in America – if the loyal Speranza was to be believed. On 18 September 1882 she wrote excitedly 'You are still the talk of London – the cabmen ask me if I am anything to Oscar Wilde – the milkman has bought your picture! and in fact nothing seems celebrated in London but you. I think you will be mobbed when you come back by eager crowds and will be obliged to shelter in cabs.'

From Novia Scotia in October Wilde had written 'I long to get back to real literary work, for although my audiences are most appreciative, I can not write while flying from one railway to another and from the cast-iron stove of one hotel to its twin horror in the next.' But in fact though his lecture tour finished in mid-October, he stayed on in America, to welcome Lillie Langtry ('dressed as probably no grown man in the world was ever dressed before,' chided the *New York Times*) – to whom he paid the compliment 'I would rather have discovered Mrs Langtry than have discovered America'. He also engaged in unsuccessful negotiations about the production of his plays. However, on 27 December 1882, Oscar Wilde finally set sail for London. 'I have had a delightful time all through California and Colorado and am now returning home twice as affected as ever...'

A month later he was off again, bound this time for Paris. In the French capital he stayed in the Hôtel Voltaire. He dressed each day in a white wool dressing-gown (the garb, as he understood, of Balzac) and tried to finish his play *The Duchess of Padua*. He started work again on an earlier poem, 'The Sphinx', and worked at his poetry with scrupulous delicacy. 'I was working on the proof of one of my poems all the morning,' he reported, 'and took out a comma...in the afternoon...I put it back in again.' He finished *The Duchess of Padua* and sent it off to Mary Anderson, a young American actress, on 23 March 1883, following it up with the conviction that 'I have no hesitation in saying that it is the masterpiece of all my literary work, the *chef d'œuvre* of my youth'. There was no response for some time, and then a letter arrived at the end of April:

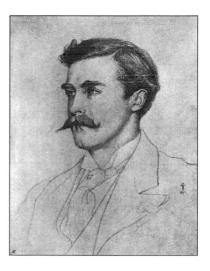

ABOVE: *A sketch of James Rennell Rodd, a fellow Newdigate Prize winner. In the summer of 1882 Wilde helped to arrange for Rodd's volume of poetry to be published in America. Wilde also wrote the dedication: 'To Oscar Wilde - heart's brother - these few songs and many songs to come'. It was a sentiment that Rodd, who was about to enter the diplomatic service, regarded as 'too effusive'. It was the end of the friendship.*

Oscar Wilde

Dear Mr Wilde,…The play in its present form, I fear, would no more please the public today than would 'Venice Preserved' or Lucretia Borgia'.
Neither of us can afford failure now, and your Duchess in my hands would not succeed, as the part does not fit me.
My admiration of your ability is as great as ever…

Wilde also consorted with a prostitute who was later murdered – 'what animals we all are,' he mused – and it was in Paris that he probably wrote his poem 'The Harlot's House':

> We caught the tread of dancing feet
> We loitered in the moonlight street,
> And stopped beneath the harlot's house
> …turning to my love, I said,
> 'The dead are dancing with the dead,
> The dust is whirling with the dust…'

Wilde also went out into literary Parisian society. He was invited to an evening reception at the house of Victor Hugo, and to the house of Edmond de Goncourt, he saw Sarah Bernhardt in the title role of Sardou's *Fédora* which had a plot disconcertingly similar to *Vera*, and he met the young man who was to be his first biographer. Robert Sherard was young and blond – and a great grandson of Wordsworth. It was an intense relationship. Sherard later recalled: 'On that first night in Paris, he appeared to me one of the most wonderful beings that I had ever met…I spent several hours in his company. I knew him brilliant beyond description – and be it remembered that I was then living in a circle of the most brilliant conversationalists in Europe, for I was an *habitué* of Victor Hugo's house, where one met everybody who counted…'

LEFT:*A photograph of Sarah Bernhardt. The most famous actress of her generation, Wilde saw her star in Racine's* Phèdre *and ever afterwards wanted her to appear in one of his plays. When he was in Paris in 1893, he called on her several times, once purchasing from a street hawker a large heap of wallflowers, which he presented to her. 'It was a poor offering,' recalled Robert Sherard, 'but she seemed delighted.'*

RIGHT:*The Boulevard in front of the Variety Theatre by Jean Beraud. Wilde relished the excitement of the Parisian theatre scene; he seized the opportunity to see Sarah Bernhardt perform in Sardou's* Fédora *during his visit*

CHAPTER 3

'THE ARTIST CAN
EXPRESS EVERYTHING'

LEFT: *Lindsey Wharf, Chelsea, by Walter Greaves. The figure of Whistler can be seen walking in the foreground. Greaves came from a family of boatmen and would row Whistler on the Thames so the artist could study the effect of light on water. Wilde lived in Chelsea for most of his adult life. His son, Vyvyan, remembered that Tite Street 'was a peculiar social mix in those days. Both [the artists] Whistler and Sargent had their studios there...and, by an ironical coincidence, at No. 46 lived Mr Justice Wills, who was to pronounce sentence on my father at the Old Bailey in 1895. On the other hand, the west side of the steet backed onto Paradise Walk, at that time one of the most forbidding of Chelsea slums.'*

'**I** am going to be married to a beautiful girl called Constance Lloyd,' wrote Oscar Wilde to Lillie Langtry, who was appearing in a play in Washington, in the middle of December 1883, 'a grave, slight, violet-eyed little Artemis, with great coils of heavy brown hair which make her flower-like head droop like a blossom, and wonderful ivory hands which draw music from the piano so sweet that the birds stop singing to listen to her. We are to be married in April. I hope so much that you will be over then. I am so anxious for you to know and to like her.'

Wilde was nearly thirty. A cruel, anonymous profile of him (written by a former fellow student at Oxford, Courtenay Bodley) had appeared in the *New York Times* as Wilde arrived for his American lecture tour in January 1882. It had branded him as 'epicene' and concluded with the observation:

..he has considerable ability, and he has seen fit to use it in obtaining a cheap notoriety; he is good-hearted, has been amusing, and probably retains some sense of humour. Will American society encourage him in the line he has taken which can only lead to one end, or will it teach him not unkindly a needed lesson and bid him return home to ponder it in growing wiser?

Nearly two years later Wilde's identity was still fluid. He was not widely recognized as a poet of any distinction, nor had any of his plays been a success yet (*Vera* had been put on in New York in August 1883, but had closed after a week). The question of the Polish actress Madame Modjeska 'but what has he *done*?' continued to retain a certain validity. If in America he had constructed himself as the spectacle of the aesthetic, in Paris he had skirted the attraction of the decadent, meeting Paul Bourget, who was

ABOVE: *A pencil sketch of Wilde by Alexander Boyd, 1883. It was probably made whilst Wilde was lecturing in Glasgow. 'It is horrid being so much away from her [Constance], but we telegraph to each other twice a day,' Wilde wrote.*

writing a book on decadence in contemporary literature, being introduced to Verlaine, immersing himself in the dark writings of Baudelaire, Rollinat, Chatterton, Mallarmé – and, of course, Edgar Allan Poe – and quoting from Nerval. He had pontificated to Robert Sherard, who was contemplating marriage: 'In England, great men love nothing, neither art, nor wealth, nor glory…nor women', and after an evening spent with him in Paris, Edmond de Goncourt had confided to his diary that in his opinion Wilde was *'au sexe douteux'*.

He had lived for a year by lecturing to America, and was now having to milk that experience to live: lecturing about America to English audiences. 'He is lecturing still,' wrote Constance's brother, Otho, 'going from town to town, but in the funniest way, one day he is at Brighton, the next he will be in Edinburgh, the next at Penzance in Cornwall, the next in Dublin' – though he was not 'getting rich' on the proceeds as he had boasted to Lillie Langtry. Indeed a magazine report of Wilde's lecture on 'Impressions of America' delivered at the Prince's Hall on 11 July, 1883, carried the headline 'Exit Oscar' and maintained that the hall was only half full.

Wilde might have proclaimed that he was now in his 'second period', but it was unclear what this transformation meant other than in the department of coiffure, as the *World* put it:

> O,
>
> *He has changed who was once so fair!*
> *Has the iron gone into his soul? O no!*
> *It has only gone over his hair.*

But Wilde had resolved on a more thorough-going change to his life. He played court to beautiful older women who were flattered by his attention, and charmed by his theatricality. He thought he would have liked to marry Florrie Balcombe, and probably had somewhat sluggish marital intentions towards 'the sweetest violet in England', Violet Hunt, the daughter of the painter Alfred William Hunt and the writer Margaret Hunt, and later a

BROTHER WILLIE.—"NEVER MIND, OSCAR; OTHER GREAT MEN HAVE HAD THEIR DRAMATIC FAILURES!"

LEFT: A cartoon by Alfred Bryan showing the not yet successful playwright in 1883. It shows Oscar Wilde being comforted by his brother Willie when his first play, Vera: or the Nihilists *failed to be produced. Max Beerbohm was not taken with Willie. 'Quel monstre! Dark, oily, suspect yet awfully like Oscar: he has Oscar's coy, carnal smile and fatuous giggle and not a little of Oscar's esprit. But he is awful – a veritable tragedy of family-likeness!'*

'THE ARTIST CAN EXPRESS EVERYTHING'

ABOVE: *A photograph of Constance Wilde in 1894. Before they had married, Constance had written to Oscar 'I don't think I shall ever be jealous. Certainly I am not jealous now of any-one: I trust in you for the present: I am content to let the past be buried, it does not belong to me: for the future trust and faith will come, and when I have you for my husband, I will hold you fast with chains of love.' Yet within little more than two years of marriage, Oscar had effectively slipped his chains.*

novelist herself, and also towards Charlotte Montefiore, whose brother had been a contemporary of Wilde at Oxford. In his as yet unwritten play *An Ideal Husband,* the character of Lord Caversham expostulates:

> Damme, sir, it is your duty to get married. You can't always be living for pleasure. Every man of position is married nowadays. Bachelors are not fashionable any more. They are a damaged lot. Too much is known about them. You must get a wife, sir.

Oscar Wilde had met Constance Lloyd at a family friend's house in London in May 1881. Constance was then twenty four and living with her grandfather, John Lloyd, Q.C., and her aunt, Emily, at 100 Lancaster Gate. She was intelligent, interested in music and art (she attended art school for a time), she embroidered and read – in Italian as well as English – and the two young people met sporadically when Oscar was in London over the next two years. On his return from Paris in May 1883 Oscar invited Constance to visit his mother's house, and by mid-summer Lady Wilde suspected that the relationship would develop. In November Wilde was in Dublin giving a series of lectures: Constance was in Dublin too, staying with her maternal grandparents in Ely Place. It was there, on 25 November 1883, in the drawing room where her father had proposed to her mother some thirty years before, that Wilde proposed to Constance and was accepted.

The couple seemed to share interests, if not to be in full agreement about their significance. Oscar had sent Constance *Vera* to read and she considered it carefully in her response:

> I was much interested…it seems to me to be a very good acting play and to have good dramatic situations…I cannot understand why you should have been so unfortunate in its reception unless either the acting was very inferior or the audience was unsympathetic to the political opinions expressed in it. The world surely is unjust and bitter to most of us; I think we must either renounce our opinions and run with the general stream or else totally ignore

ABOVE: *16, Tite Street. Built in the late fifties or early sixties of the nineteenth century, '[it] was more spacious inside than [its] frontage led one to expect'. An example of speculative housing, the new tenants, Mr and Mrs Oscar Wilde, set about having the property transformed by the same architect as Whistler had employed, E.W. Godwin. The costly redecoration of the 'House Beautiful' soon meant that 'money is as scarce as sunlight'.*

the world and go on our own regardless of all, there is not the slightest use in *fighting* against existing prejudices, for we are only worsted in the struggle – I am afraid you and I disagree in our opinions on art, for I hold that there is no perfect art without perfect morality, whilst you say that they are distinct and separable things, and of course you have your knowledge to combat my ignorance with. Truly I am no judge that you should appeal to me for opinions, and even if I were, I know that I should judge you rather by your aims than by your work, and you would say I was wrong.

And Wilde wrote to the American sculptor, Waldo Story: '*Her* name is Constance and she is quite young, very grave and mystical, with wonderful eyes, and dark brown coils of hair: quite perfect except that she does not think Jimmy [Whistler] the only painter that ever existed: she would like to bring Titian or somebody in by the back door: however, she knows I am the greatest poet, so in literature she is all right…We are, of course, desperately in love.' However, as a prospective grandson-in-law Wilde evidently left something to be desired: notably the wherewithal to keep Miss Lloyd in the manner to which she was accustomed – or even in financial solvency. Wilde was considerably in debt, and Constance's grandfather proposed that the marriage should be postponed until the debt was reduced. At present Constance had an income of £250 a year: when John Lloyd died it would increase to £900 a year and against this expectation £5,000 was advanced to the betrothed couple to lease and furnish a house.

On 29 May 1884 Oscar Wilde and Constance Lloyd were married at St James's Church, Sussex Gardens, near Paddington. The bride's grandfather was ill – he died in July, thus freeing up Miss Lloyd's inheritance – so the wedding was small and quiet. Nevertheless Constance looked beautiful as befitted an aesthete's bride, in a dress of 'rich creamy satin' of 'a delicate cowslip tint; the bodice cut square and somewhat low in front, was finished with a high Medici collar'; the skirt was 'gathered by a silver girdle of beautiful workmanship' – a gift from the groom; and the whole ensemble was

LEFT: *A sketch from one of Godwin's notebooks showing furniture in the Japanese style. Wilde was delighted with the designs for Tite Street: 'I enclose a cheque and thank you very much for the beautiful designs of the furniture…Each chair is a sonnet in ivory, and the table is a masterpiece in pearl…the white furniture reminds us of you daily, and we find a rose leaf can be laid on the ivory table without scratching – at least a white one can. That is something.'*

LEFT: Aesthetic Woman in Rational Dress *by E.W. Godwin. Wilde profoundly believed in the translation of the aesthetic into daily life: 'People's appreciation of beauty depends so much on what they see around them...We want to see the homes of the people beautiful, and when that is the case people will no longer talk of the beautiful at all.' Godwin's painting epitomized many ideas of aesthetic design, including blue and white china and decorated panels, and illustrates the fashion parodied by Gilbert in* Patience *'for all one sees / that's Japanese'.*

topped with a veil of 'saffron-coloured Indian gauze…embroidered with pearls and worn Marie Stuart fashion: a thick wreath of myrtle leaves, through which gleamed a few white blossoms, crowned [the bride's] fair, frizzed hair; the dress was ornamented with clusters of myrtle leaves; the large bouquet had as much green in it as white.' Lady Wilde looked splendid in grey satin and 'a luxuriant plume of ostrich feathers'.

The couple spent their honeymoon in Paris staying, as Constance wrote to her brother, in 'an *appartement* of three rooms, twenty francs a day: not dear for a Paris hotel: we are *au quatrième* and have a lovely view over the gardens of the Tuileries.' Sherard called on them on the second morning – Constance thought he had 'a romantic face' – and the two men took a walk together, Sherard only just managing to restrain Wilde from telling him in graphic detail the delights of the nuptial bed. A week later Wilde informed a reporter that he was 'too happy to be interviewed', but allowed himself to be anyway and talked of Sarah Bernhardt. Mr and Mrs Wilde returned to London on 24 June, but it was another six months before their house at 16 [now 34] Tite Street, a few doors from where Wilde had roomed with Frank Miles, was ready. The design was again entrusted to the architect Edward Godwin and it was to be like Whistler's house – white or largely white, with a white painted front door and frosted glass panels. The four-storey terrace house had a library on the ground floor where Wilde smoked, talked and wrote. It was richly decorated in Moorish or Turkish style and over the doorway was an inscription from Shelley:

Spirit of Beauty! Tarry still awhile,
They are not dead, thine ancient votaries,
Some few there are to whom thy radiant smile
Is better than a thousand victories.

On the mantelpiece of a drawing room on the second floor of the 'House Beautiful' stood a small bronze of Narcissus; and in the corner stood the marble bust of Augustus that Wilde had received when he was awarded the

LEFT: *A sketch of the French actress Sarah Bernhardt by Sir Robert Ponsonby-Staples. 'Wilde and Constance saw her play Lady Macbeth on their honeymoon in Paris; Constance commented: 'the witches were charmingly grotesque, the Macbeth very good, Sarah, of course, superb, she simply stormed the part.'*

Newdigate Prize at Oxford. Originally the ceiling was painted with gold dragons by Whistler, but these later made room for peacock feathers stuck in the plaster cornices.

The Wildes settled down to a certain pattern of existence. Constance had toyed with the idea of a career: 'I am thinking of becoming a correspondent to some paper, or else of going on the stage: *qu'en pensez vous?* I want to make some money: perhaps a novel would be better,' she wrote to her brother, Otho. In the meantime Oscar made what money he could by continuing to travel the country giving lectures – and writing home to Constance in classic mode:

> Dear and Beloved, Here I am, and you at the Antipodes. O execrable facts that keep our lips from kissing, though our souls are one.
>
> What can I tell you by letter? Alas! nothing that I would tell you. The messages of the gods travel to each other not by pen and ink and indeed your bodily presence here would not make you more real: for I feel your fingers in my hair, and your cheek brushing mine. The air is full of the music of your voice, my soul and body seem no longer mine, but mingled in some exquisite ecstasy with yours. I feel incomplete without you. Ever and ever yours…Oscar

He had added a new lecture to his repertoire on 'Impressions of America' (now renamed 'The Value of Art in Modern Life') concerning 'Dress.' He experimented on Constance who, it was noted by his friends, might turn up at social occasions wearing a pale yellow and apple green Greek costume, or maybe 'a limp white muslin with *no* bustle, saffron coloured silk swathed about her shoulders, a huge cartwheel Gainsborough hat, white and yellow stockings and shoes'. When she attended a meeting of the Rational Dress Society in March 1886 at Westminster Town Hall, she was attired in cinnamon cashmere trousers and a cape caught under the arms to form sleeves – an outfit which the satirical magazine *The Bat* pronounced 'strictly irrational'. In his lectures her husband drew for inspiration as

RIGHT: *A cartoon of Richard Le Gallienne by Max Beerbohm, 1896. Wilde met the poet in 1883, when he was seventeen and came to hear one of his lectures in Birkenhead. A friendship soon developed:*

> With Oscar Wilde a summer-day
> Passed like a yearning kiss away

wrote Le Gallienne, who was to become a frequent visitor to Tite Street. Enraptured by Oscar, he claimed to find Constance 'evangelically religious' and somewhat humourless.

RICHARD · LE · GALLIENNE   MAX

RIGHT: Nocturne in Blue and Gold —
Old Battersea Bridge *by James McNeill
Whistler, 1887. Whistler and Wilde had
long been intellectual sparring partners;
Wilde declared the painting to be 'worth
looking at for about as long as one looks at
a real rocket, that is less than a quarter of
a minute'. Whistler defended his painting
as being 'intended simply as a
representation of moonlight' and mocked
Wilde's credentials as an artist and a
critic: 'What has Oscar in common with
Art? except that he dines at our tables and
picks from our platters the plums for the
pudding he peddles in the provinces.'*

ABOVE: *Illustrations from 'Children's Dress in This Century', one of the two articles that Constance contributed to* Woman's World *under her husband's editorship. She wrote that 'the greater number of children are undoubtedly dressed more simply, more rationally, more like human sentient beings, less like wooden dolls, or dummies to wear the freaks of fancy dictated by dressmakers' than earlier in the century.*

usual on the classical world and advocated clothes hung from the shoulder rather than the waist. He also recommended that women should forego bustles and corsets, and high heels which threw them forward.

All this by-passing of the waist would have been very suitable for Constance, who was pregnant. The Wildes' first child, Cyril, was born on 5 June 1885, a little over a year after their marriage, and a second son, Vyvyan, on 5 November 1886. Soon Oscar's room in Tite Street, with its plaster cast of the Hermes of Praxiteles, was given over to serve as the children's bedroom and his study, decorated in shades of red and vermilion (which he pronounced emphasizing the usually silent 'l') became part of the day and night nurseries on the second floor.

His friend, the writer and editor of *Fortnightly Review*, Frank Harris, claimed that Wilde had told him:

> When I married, my wife was a beautiful girl, white and slim as a lily, with dancing eyes and gay rippling laughter like music. In a year or so the flowerlike grace had all vanished; she became heavy, shapeless, deformed. She dragged herself about the house in uncouth misery with drawn, blotched face and hideous body, sick at heart because of our love. It was dreadful. I tried to be kind to her; forced myself to touch and kiss her; but she was sick always, and – oh! I cannot recall it, it is all loathsome…I used to wash my mouth and open the window to cleanse my lips in the pure air.

He continued to live with Constance at Tite Street: he was fond of her, she was loving and admiring of him. They entertained ('Wednesdays is our day') and went out together in society, and he took pleasure in his children. 'The baby is wonderful,' he had written to Forbes Robertson when Cyril was born, 'it has a bridge to its nose! which the nurse says is a proof of genius! It also has a superb voice which it freely exercises: its style is essentially Wagnerian.' Other friends worried about the fate of an aesthete's infant – 'Will it be swathed in artistic baby clothes? Sage green bibs and tuckers, I suppose, and a peacock blue robe.' But increasingly Wilde was

ABOVE: *A sketch of Constance with the Wildes' elder son, Cyril, illustrating an article on 'Little-known Wives of Well-known Men' in the magazine* Home Notes, *19 May 1894. When* The Happy Prince and Other Tales *was published in May 1888, Wilde explained that 'It is the duty of every father to write fairy tales for his children.' When he read one of his stories to Cyril, he explained that he had tears in his eyes because 'really beautiful things' always made him cry.*

absent from home, and as far as the marriage was concerned, he embraced celibacy.

As a family man with a habit of unstinting generosity both to himself and to his friends, the matter of money pressed heavily. 'Believe me, that it is impossible to live by literature,' wrote Wilde to an unknown young man in 1885. 'By journalism a man may make an income, but rarely by pure literary work…I would strongly advise you to try and make some profession, such as that of tutor, the basis and mainstay of your life, and to keep literature for your finest, rarer moments. The best work in literature is always done by those who do not depend upon it for their daily bread, and the highest form of literature, poetry, brings no wealth to the singer.'

It was not until the spring of 1887 that the possibility of a regular income materialized when Wilde was approached by the general manager of the publishing house of Cassell, Thomas Wemyss Reid. The previous autumn Cassell had launched a new monthly magazine, entitled *The Lady's World*. With a cover price of one shilling, the publication was subtitled a 'Magazine of Fashion and Society'. The early issues were primarily concerned with the latest 'dress and fashion of the highest class', interspersed with 'the doings of Society at home and abroad.' By the following spring Wemyss Reid realized that the initial formula was not working; to revitalize the magazine, he cast around for a new and original editor. He sent Wilde some back issues to peruse. Wilde responded in April:

LEFT: *A pen and ink sketch of Constance Wilde at a charity bazaar. 'Endowed by nature with great beauty of form and colouring, Mrs Wilde seems admirably fitted to be the wife of a man so devoted to Art and all that is beautiful,' eulogized the magazine* Home Notes. *Constance was also committed to the practical and was a supporter — and exemplar — of Rational Dress for women.*

'THE ARTIST CAN EXPRESS EVERYTHING'

I have read very carefully the numbers of the *Lady's World* you kindly sent me, and would be very happy to join with you in the work of editing and to some extent reconstructing it. It seems to me that at present it is too feminine and not sufficiently womanly. No one appreciates more fully than I do the value and importance of Dress, in its relation to good taste and good health: indeed the subject is one that I have constantly lectured on before Institutes and Societies of various kinds...we should take a wider range, as well as a high standpoint, and deal not merely with what women wear, but with what they think, and what they feel. *The Lady's World* should be made the recognised organ for the expression of women's opinions on all subjects of literature, art and modern life, and yet it should be a magazine that men could read with pleasure, and consider it a privilege to contribute ...we should not rely exclusively on women, even for signed articles: artists have sex but art has none, and now and then an article by some man of letters would be of service...From time to time also we must have news from Girton and Newnham Colleges at Cambridge, and from Oxford colleges.

Wilde set to work to transform the magazine: 'Dear Miss Nellie,' he wrote to Helena Sickert on 27 May 1887:

I am going to become an Editor (for my sins or my virtues?) and want you to write me an article. The magazine will try to be representative of the thought and culture of the women of this century, and I am very anxious that those who have had university training like yourself, should have an organ through which they can express their views on life and things

On 5 September 1887 Wilde wrote again to Wemyss Reid:

I am very anxious that you should make a final appeal to the Directors to alter the name of the magazine I am to edit for them from the *Lady's World* to the *Woman's World*. The present name of the magazine has a certain taint of vulgarity about it...and is also extremely misleading...

ABOVE: *The logo of Cassell & Company Limited, publishers of* The Woman's World. *'The position [of editor] was perhaps one of the most extraordinary ever occupied in Oscar Wilde's extraordinary career...True, it only incurred his attendance at* La Belle Sauvage *[the Cassell offices off Ludgate Hill] twice a week – on the mornings of Tuesday and Thursday – but the very fact that regularity in any form became a factor in his life seemed an incongruity,' marvelled his assistant editor, Arthur Fish.*

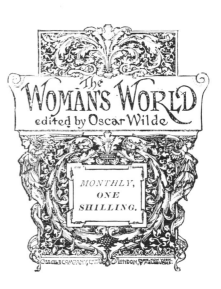

ABOVE: *An advertisment for* The Woman's World *in 1887. 'I have been asked to become literary advisor to one of the monthly magazines, and I hope to make it the organ through which women of culture and position will be able to express their views.' As the new editor, Wilde wrote to a host of just such women – including one who had suggested an article on 'Playing at Botany', which idea he embraced with enthusiasm.*

The editor got his way, and later that month was writing enthusiastically to Harriet Hamilton, the poet and ardent supporter of Italian independence: 'I think you will find that the *Woman's World* will be a really intellectual and cultured magazine. It will be quite different from the *Lady's World*, which seems to me to have been a very vulgar, trivial and stupid production, with its silly gossip about silly people, and its social inanities.'

The first issue was published at the end of November 1887 – with a new masthead, redesigned pink cover and with Wilde's name on the title page. The relaunched magazine was a success at first. Its 'keynote' was 'the right of woman to equality of treatment with man, with the assertion of her claims by women who had gained high position by virtue of their skill as writers or workers in the world's great field of labour.' Wilde managed to attract a range of talented writers – largely women and including his mother, who at the time was editing his late father's notes on Irish folklore, and his wife, who contributed an article on muffs and another on dress for children. However, Queen Victoria, when solicited for a poem, indicated that 'never…in her whole life' had she written 'one line of poetry serious or comic or make a Rhyme even'.

At first Wilde was an active and assiduous editor. His assistant, Arthur Fish, found him 'extraordinary'. But soon the discipline chafed: after a few months his arrival time became later and his departure time earlier, until at times his visit was 'little more than a call'. It had been agreed that the editor would contribute 'Literary and Other Notes', but these tailed off after the first four issues. Fish noted that 'oftentimes the press day found the

LEFT: *A pastel chalk sketch of Charles Ricketts and Charles Shannon by William Rothenstein, c.1890. Wilde found Charles Ricketts 'very interesting and cultivated'. He and his lifelong companion Charles Shannon were jointly or separately the designer and illustrator of many of Wilde's books and plays.*

RIGHT: *'Melancholia', Ricketts' design for the frontispiece of 'The Sphinx', 1894. The 'riddle' of the mythological creature — half-woman, half-lion, with the wings of a bird and a serpent's tail — ran:*

> What goes on four feet,
> On two feet and three,
> But the more feet it goes on
> The weaker it be?

The answer was Man, in the successive phases of his life.

THE SPHINX BY OSCAR WILDE

MEL·
AN·
CHO·
LIA·

WITH DECORATIONS BY CHARLES RICKETTS
LONDON MDCCCXCIV
ELKIN MATHEWS AND JOHN LANE . AT THE SIGN OF THE BODLEY HEAD,
BOSTON
COPELAND AND DAY LXIX CORNHILL

printers awaiting "copy" for the pages left for the editor to fill' and he would receive a note: 'I have not been at all well and cannot get my notes done. Can you manage to put in something else? I will be down tomorrow. – Truly yours O.W.' The magazine was losing circulation, and in March 1889, the directors of Cassell, apparently somewhat reluctantly, gave the editor one described as 'so indolent, but such a genius', six months notice. The magazine then took on a more practical, down-market character, in which guise it competed unsuccessfully for readers with the plethora of new women's magazines – including the highly successful *Home Chat* from the stable of new press baron, Alfred Harmsworth. *The Woman's World* finally ceased publication in 1890.

Arthur Fish, whom Wilde came to think of 'as one of my real friends', had perceptively described Wilde's editorship as a case of 'Pegasus in harness'. Routine did not suit Wilde – either at work: 'I have known men come to London full of bright prospects and seen them complete wrecks in a few months through a habit of answering letters,' he told Fish; nor in the conjugal home. He would quote Walter Pater: 'Failure is to form habits'.

The less-than-ideal husband was fixated on sensation. At the beginning of 1886 Wilde was staying at the Central Hotel, Glasgow, probably whilst lecturing in Scotland. He wrote in a letter:

> You too have the love of things impossible…*l'amour de l'impossible* (how do men name it?) Sometimes you will find, even as I have found, that there is no such thing as a romantic experience; there are romantic memories, and there is the desire of romance – that is all. Our most fiery moments of ecstasy are merely shadows of what somewhere else we have felt, or of what we long some day to feel. So at least it seems to me. And, strangely enough, what comes of all this is a curious mixture of ardour and of indifference. I myself would sacrifice everything for a new experience, and I know there is no such thing as a new experience at all. I think I would more readily die for what I do not believe in than for what I hold to be true. I would go to the

ABOVE: *In his role as editor of* The Woman's World, *Wilde would turn up twice a week at the offices off Ludgate Hill at about 11am, having travelled by underground from Sloane Square. He was by far 'the best dressed man in the establishment'…wearing 'in winter a long fur-lined coat with heavy fur collar and cuffs; in summer a pale-grey frock-coat suit'…on his cheerful days there would be 'a buttonhole of Parma violets'.*

TO

CONSTANCE MARY WILDE.

ABOVE: *Oscar Wilde's second book of fairy tales,* The House of Pomegranates, *published in 1891, was dedicated to Constance. Speranza was enthusiastic: 'Caro Figlio Mio' [My dear son],' she wrote, 'Your book is beautiful, most beautiful…Jewels of thought set in the fine gold of the most exquisite words…Constance is much pleased at the dedication to her…You have quite taught this age the meaning of a beautiful book.'*

THE STAR-CHILD ⚘ ⚘ ⚘.

TO
MISS MARGOT TENNANT.

ONCE upon a time two poor Woodcutters were making their way home through a great pine-forest. It was winter, and a night of bitter cold. The snow lay thick upon the ground, and upon the branches of the trees : the frost kept snapping the little twigs on either side of them, as they passed : and when they came to the Moun-tain-Torrent she was hang-ing motionless in air, for the Ice-King had kissed her.

So cold was it that even the animals and the birds did not know what to make of it.

" Ugh ! " snarled the

S 129

RIGHT: Nocturne in Black and Gold: The Falling Rocket *by Whistler. The artist and critic John Ruskin charged that Whistler's painting of a firework display in the Cremorne Gardens, Chelsea, was 'slapdash', the equivalent 'of flinging a pot of paint in the public's face'. Whistler sued for libel in 1878 and was awarded a farthing damages and no costs. The case precipitated his bankruptcy and he fled for a while to Venice. The title of his book* The Gentle Art of Making Enemies *(1890) spoke both of Whistler's temperament and of his ability to disturb artistic complacencies.*

ABOVE: *Whistler's distinctive 'butterfly' motif. Its genesis was in Whistler's monogram J.W., but the design evolved and changed, and soon became recognized by Press and public as the artist's signature. The butterfly sometimes anthropomorphized — according to its status. Sometimes it resembled the artist and when Whistler wrote to the Press — as he did frequently — a sting in the tail was added.*

RIGHT: *'But nobody heard him, not even the two boys, for they were asleep.' An illustration by Walter Crane for Wilde's fairy story 'The Remarkable Rocket', first published in 1888. Wilde's allegory on Whistler and the pyrotechnics of his libel case against Ruskin over* The Falling Rocket *was another stage in their artistic confrontation. 'You should be thinking about me,' [said the Rocket] ' I am always thinking about myself and I expect everyone else to do the same...I am going to set the whole world on fire, and make such a noise that nobody will talk about anything else for a whole year...'*

stake for a sensation and be a sceptic to the last. Only one thing remains infinitely fascinating to me, the mystery of moods. To be master of these moods is exquisite, to be mastered by them, more exquisite still. Sometimes I think that the artistic life is a long and lovely suicide, and I am not sorry that it is so.

And much of this I fancy you yourself have felt: much also remains for you to feel. There is an unknown land full of strange flowers and subtle perfumes, a land of which it is joy of all joys to dream, a land where all things are perfect and poisonous.

The letter was to Harry Marillier, 'the bright enthusiastic boy who used to bring me my coffee', and whom Wilde had tutored in Greek in the house shared with Frank Miles in Salisbury Street five years before. Marillier was now an undergraduate at Peterhouse, Cambridge, and had written to invite Wilde to come to see a performance of the Greek tragedy *Eumenides* the previous November. Wilde was entranced to hear from him and seized the hope that Marillier would combine the two things he found most compelling: youth and decadence. 'I wish you were here Harry,' he was to write, 'I have never learned anything except from people younger than myself and you are infinitely young.' And from Newcastle he wrote to the young man he had left behind in London:

Harry, why did you let me catch my train? I would like to have gone to the National Gallery with you, and looked at Velasquez's pale evil King, at Titian's Bacchus with velvet panthers, and at that strange heaven of Angelico's where everyone seems made of gold and purple and fire, and which, for all that, looks to me ascetic – everyone dead and decorative. I wonder if it will

LEFT: *An illustration by Paul Thiriot from the first illustrated edition of* The Picture of Dorian Gray, *published in Paris in 1908. 'It is your best work, Basil, it is the best thing you have ever done,' said Lord Henry, languidly. 'You must certainly send it next year to the Grosvenor'... 'I know you will laugh at me,' [Basil Hallward] replied, 'but I really can't exhibit it. I have put too much of myself into it.'*

RIGHT: *A photograph by 'Baron Corvo' (Frederick Rolfe) which accompanied an article on 'The Nude in Photography' in* The Studio *art magazine. The fascination of youthful beauty is integral to* The Picture of Dorian Gray, *which describes the protagonist as a 'young Adonis, who looks as if he was made out of ivory and rose leaves...He is a narcissus...beauty, real beauty, ends where intellectual expression begins'.*

really be like that, but I wonder without caring...If I do live again I would like it to be as a flower – no soul but perfectly beautiful. Perhaps for my sins I shall be made a red geranium!'

It was an intense and sensate yearning, but it was unconsummated. Wilde revelled in the gestures of homosexuality: he was less sanguine about its realities. Some ten years earlier he had seen a fellow Oxford student at a Dublin theatre sitting with a choirboy in a private box. He had written pragmatically to William Ward: 'Myself, I believe Todd is extremely moral and only mentally spoons the boy, but I think he is foolish to go about with one, if he *is* bringing this boy about with him. You are the only one I would tell about it, as you have a philosophical mind...'

But later in 1886 Wilde met Robert Ross, who was being crammed for Cambridge. With his Puck-like face, Ross looked younger than his seventeen years. Wilde was thirty-two. Ross, the grandson of the Governor General of Canada, seduced Wilde, and they were lovers, then friends, for the rest of Wilde's life. As Wilde realized his sensuality in his relationships with Ross, and other young men such as Richard Le Gallienne (to whom Wilde presented a copy of his poems inscribed 'To Richard Le Gallienne, poet and lover, from Oscar Wilde', and to whom he wrote: 'Friendship and love like ours need no meetings, but they are delightful. I hope the laurels are not too thick across your brow for me to kiss your eyelids'), so did he realize his sensual aestheticism in his writings. The culmination of this theme was to be *The Picture of Dorian Gray*.

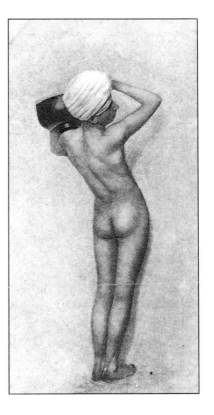

> Art takes life as part of her rough material, recreates it, and refashions it in
> fresh forms, is absolutely indifferent to fact, invents, imagines, dreams and
> keeps between herself and reality the impenetrable barrier of beautiful style,
> of decorative or ideal treatment.

Wilde had styled himself as an aesthete, a tentative Catholic convert, a husband, a poet, a lecturer, a journalist, a playwright. He would visit these

ABOVE: *A pen and ink caricature of Wilde by Beatrice Whistler, wife of the artist James McNeill Whistler.*

manifestations again, and all were part of his formation as a writer, the occasions of his wit, the material for his self-plagiarism. By the end of the 1880s his media were essays, articles, short stories – and then novels. 'The Portrait of Mr W.H.' was written in 1887, but not published until July 1889 in *Blackwood's* magazine. It concerned the age-old conundrum about 'the subject of the identity of the young man to whom [Shakespeare's] sonnets are addressed': for Wilde the identity was that of the boy actor Willie Hughes. 'You *must* believe in Willie Hughes,' he told Helena Sickert, 'I almost do myself.' He commissioned the artist Charles Ricketts to paint a portrait of Hughes, and continued to experiment with form and purpose in discussing the role of art and the artist, giving himself a role in its definition through a series of articles: 'To those who are pre-occupied with the beauty of form, nothing else seems of much importance'; 'The telling of beautiful untrue things is the proper aim of art'; 'All art is immoral?' 'Yes. For emotion for the sake of emotion is the aim of art, and emotion for the sake of action is the aim of life'; 'Nobody of any real culture talks about the beauty of sunsets. Sunsets are quite old fashioned. To admire them is a distinct sign of provincialism.' As with his lectures and magazine journalism, once Wilde had started to write in a medium his industry and output were prodigious.

The essays that had first appeared in The *Nineteenth Century* and The *Fortnightly Review* – 'The Truth of Masks', 'Pen, Pencil and Poison', 'The Decay of Lying' and 'The Critic as Artist' were republished in book form as *Intentions*. This attracted interest and criticism, but it was to be overshadowed by Wilde's longest prose narrative that first appeared as a 97-page article in *Lippincott's Monthly Magazine* on 20 June 1890. It was entitled *The Picture of Dorian Gray*.

'I have just finished my first long story, and am tired out,' Wilde wrote to a friend in early 1890. 'I am afraid it is rather like my own life – all conversation and no action. I can't describe action: my people sit in chairs and chatter...I first conceived the idea of a young man selling his soul in exchange for eternal youth – an idea that is old in the history of literature,

ABOVE: *A cartoon of Robert Ross by Max Beerbohm. Ross was to prove himself the most loyal of Wilde's companions. 'You come with the heart of Christ, and you help me intellectually as no one else can or ever could do,' wrote Wilde. After Wilde's death Ross regretted 'I am not alas a Boswell...I only met him [Wilde] in '86 and only became intimate when he was writing* Lady Windermere, *but there were long intervals when I never saw him and he never corresponded with me regularly until after his downfall.'*

'THE ARTIST CAN EXPRESS EVERYTHING'

RIGHT: *A portrait of Mallarmé by François Nardi. Wilde greatly admired the work of the symbolist poet and sent him a copy of* The Picture of Dorian Gray *in return for a gift from Mallarmé, his translation of Edgar Allan Poe's 'The Raven' into French. Mallarmé responded: 'I am finishing the book, one of the few that can take hold of the reader, since from an inner reverie and the strangest perfumes of the soul, it stirs up a storm... This full-length disquieting portrait of a Dorian Gray will haunt...'*

ABOVE: *In his collected pamphlets and letters to the press,* The Gentle Art of Making Enemies, *Whistler's butterflies 'danced, laughed, mocked, stung, defied, triumphed...' Mallarmé had great respect for Whistler, and had to negotiate a difficult situation when he also showed hospitality to Wilde. The uneasy relationship between Whistler and Wilde had become openly antagonistic.*

RIGHT: *A page from* Les Fleurs du Mal *('The Flowers of Evil') by Charles Baudelaire, 1857. 'In this dreadful book I have put all my heart, all my tenderness, all my religion (disguised), all my hatred. It is true that I shall write the contrary, that I shall swear by the great gods that it is a work of pure art.' Baudelaire's poems were to prove an inspiration for the* fin de siècle *decadents, symbolists and aesthetics – Wilde included.*

206   LES FLEURS DU MAL

CX

Une Martyre

DESSIN D'UN MAITRE INCONNU

Au milieu des flacons, des étoffes lamées
    Et des meubles voluptueux,
Des marbres, des tableaux, des robes parfumées
    Qui traînent à plis somptueux,

Dans une chambre tiède où, comme en une serre,
    L'air est dangereux et fatal,
Où des bouquets mourants dans leurs cercueils de verre
    Exhalent leur soupir final,

Un cadavre sans tête épanche, comme un fleuve,
    Sur l'oreiller désaltéré
Un sang rouge et vivant, dont la toile s'abreuve
    Avec l'avidité d'un pré.

Semblable aux visions pâles qu'enfante l'ombre
    Et qui nous enchaînent les yeux,
La tête, avec l'amas de sa crinière sombre
    Et de ses bijoux précieux,

Une Martyre.

RIGHT: *'I have kissed your mouth, Jokanaan.' An illustration by Beardsley for the French edition of* Salome, *which appeared in* The Studio *magazine in April 1893. Salomé herself was a recognized decadent icon; Beardsley's astonishing drawings conflate 'female corrosive desire and male homosexual love', and identified Wilde with Salomé. The original drawing, complete with green water wash, apparently 'aroused more horror and indignation than any graphic work hitherto produced in England', although it prompted the publisher John Lane to commission Beardsley to illustrate the English edition (several of the illustrations were later suppressed). Baudelaire called his poems* 'Fleurs du Mal'; *Wilde told Beardsley 'I shall call your drawings* Fleurs du Péché — *flowers of sin.'*

but to which I have given new form' – as the tale of a man who retains his youthful good looks as his painted image ages. 'I think it will be ultimately recognized as a real work of art with a strong ethical message in it,' predicted its author. But at the time of publication *Dorian Gray* was almost universally condemned in the press for its immorality .

The *Daily Mail* characterized it as 'a tale spawned from the leprous literature of the French *décadents* – a poisonous book, the atmosphere of which is heavy with the mephitic odours of moral and spiritual putrefaction', whilst the *Scots Observer* carried an indignant review:

> The story – which deals with matters fitted only for the Criminal Investigation Department or a hearing *in camera* – is discreditable alike to author and editor. Mr Wilde has brains, and art, and style; but if he can write for none but outlawed noblemen and perverted telegraph boys [a clear reference to the recent scandal of Cleveland Street, where the aristocratic Lord Arthur Somerset and the Earl of Euston were said to have frequented a homosexual brothel in which telegraph boys from the nearby General Post Office were alleged to have been on offer for the clients], the sooner he takes to tailoring (or some other decent trade) the better for his own reputation and public morals.

It was as if the press was readily confusing the author with his writing, subscribing to the view of Basil Hallward, the painter of Dorian Gray, 'every portrait that is painted with feeling is a portrait of the artist, not the sitter'.

In response to such charges, Wilde wrote wearily '[it] makes me despair of the possibility of any general culture in England. Were I a French author, and my book were brought out in Paris, there is not a single literary critic in France of high standing who would think for a moment of criticising it from an ethical standpoint. If he did so he would stultify himself, not merely in the eyes of all men of letters, but in the eyes of the majority of the public.'

And he set off to spend two months in Paris, meeting for the first time the young writer André Gide, who recalled:

In '91…Wilde had…the chief gift of great men: success. His gesture, his look triumphed. His success was so certain that it seemed that it preceded Wilde and all he needed to do was to go forward to meet it. His books astonished, charmed. His plays were to be the talk of London…he was handsome; laden with good fortune and honours. Some compared him to an Asiatic Bacchus; others to some Roman emperor; others to Apollo himself and the fact is that he was radiant…no sooner did he arrive, than his name ran from mouth to mouth;…I heard him spoken of at the house of Mallarmé [where he was a regular attender, like other French writers, of the poet's famous Tuesday salons]; he was portrayed as a brilliant talker.

When Gide finally met Wilde, this feeling was confirmed:

Wilde did not converse: he narrated. Throughout almost the whole of the meal, he did not stop narrating. He narrated gently, slowly, his voice was very wonderful. He knew French admirably…he had almost no accent, or at least only such as it pleased him to retain and which might give the words a sometimes new and strange aspect…Before others…Wilde wore a showy mask designed to astonish, amuse, or, at times, exasperate. He never listened, and paid scant attention to ideas as soon as they were no longer his own. As soon as he ceased to shine all by himself, he effaced himself…he was himself again only when one was once more alone with him.

ABOVE and RIGHT: Costumes designed by Charles Ricketts for a private performance of Salome *by the Literary Stage Society in June 1906. In planning his own earlier production, which was thwarted by the Lord Chamberlain's ban, Wilde had had elaborate schemes: 'a violet sky and then, in place of an orchestra, braziers of perfume. Think — the scented clouds rising and partly veiling the stage from time to time — a new perfume for each emotion.' It was not to be;* Salome *was not premièred until 1896, in Paris, and was not publicly performed in England until 1931.*

When Wilde finally left Paris, Gide was to feel eviscerated, claiming Wilde 'did me nothing but harm. In his company I lost the habit of thinking.'

As well as turning the heads of the young men of Paris, Wilde was working on his version of another scandalous story: that of Salome, who danced before King Herod carrying the severed head of John the Baptist on a platter, and kissed its lips: 'Ah! I have kissed thy mouth, Jokanaan. I have kissed thy mouth. There was a bitter taste on thy lips. Was it the taste of blood…? But perchance it is the taste of love. They say that love has a bitter taste…But what of that? What of that? I have kissed thy mouth, Jokanaan.'

RIGHT: Salome *by Gustave Moreau,*
1890. One of the many décadents
fascinated by the biblical story, Moreau
perceived Salome as a femme fatale *of the*
fin de siècle. *Wilde acknowledged*
Moreau's influence in describing his
desired illustrations for his own play:
'My Herod is like the Herod of Gustave
Moreau, wrapped in his jewels and
sorrows My Salome is a mystic, the sister
of Salammbo, a Sainte Thérèse who
worships the moon.'

CHAPTER 4

'I BECAME THE SPENDTHRIFT OF MY OWN GENIUS'

'He is quite like a narcissus – so white and gold…he lies like a hyacinth on the sofa and I worship him,' wrote Oscar Wilde in the summer of 1892 of Lord Alfred Douglas, or 'Bosie' as he was known, a childish mispronunciation of the nickname 'Boysie' carried into adult life. 'It is only shallow people,' Wilde had pronounced as an aesthetic credo in *The Picture of Dorian Gray,* 'who do not judge by appearances. The true mystery of the world is the visible, not the invisible.'

Wilde was particularly entranced by Bosie's fair hair – 'gilt' or 'honey' hair he would eulogize, and figure Bosie as a sunbeam who brightened life by its rays. Their relationship eclipsed all his earlier passions, which now seemed commonplace in comparison to his new rapture. Yet Wilde's cult of youth had led him to delight in the company of several young men. Max Beerbohm was still at school at Charterhouse when he first met Wilde in 1888. The schoolboy admired, teased and imitated Wilde, but always stayed a little detached; he was later cruelly to caricature the flamboyance of the older aesthete. More transitory interest had focused on Harry Marillier and his undergraduate circle, and the student poet Lionel Johnson, who was to write a paean in Latin entitled 'In honour of Dorian and his Creator':

> Here are the apples of Sodom;
> Here are the very hearts of vices;
> And sweet sins.
> In the heavens and in the depths,
> Be to you, who perceived so much,
> Glory of all glories.

LEFT: The Strand, London at Theatre Time, *by George Hyde Pownall. Oscar Wilde, the playwright, was to experience enormous success on the London stage. He explained to a journalist who was interviewing him about his craft: 'If a journalist is run over by a four-wheeler in the Strand, an incident I regret to say I have never witnessed, it suggests nothing to me from a dramatic point of view. Perhaps I am wrong; but the artist must have his limitations'.*

Oscar Wilde

For Johnson, the inspiration for the character of Dorian Gray was clear: 'I have made great friends with the original Dorian,' he claimed, 'a youth… aged thirty, with the face of fifteen.' The model for Dorian to whom he referred was one John Gray, an ambitious, good looking young man who worked as a clerk in the Foreign Office library. He nursed literary ambitions and was widely assumed to be a lover of Oscar's. Wilde used the budding symbolist poet's name – and his beauty – in *The Picture of Dorian Gray* – a 'scandalous' novel which both formulated, and revealed the dangers in, a philosophy of sensual aestheticism:

A RECOLLECTION:
OSCAR WILDE, CHARLES CONDER, MAX BEERBOHM AND THE WRITER
AT THE CAFE ROYAL, BY MAX

> You have a wonderfully beautiful face, Mr Gray… And Beauty is a form of Genius – is higher, indeed, than Genius as it needs no explanation. It is one of the great facts of the world, like sunlight, or spring-time, or the reflection in dark waters of that silver shell we call the moon… It makes princes of those that have it… To me beauty is the wonder of wonders. It is only shallow people who do not judge by appearances. The true mystery of the world is the visible, not the invisible… Yes, Mr Gray, the Gods have been good to you. But what the Gods give they quickly take away. You have only a few years in which to live really, perfectly, and fully… Ah! realise your youth while you have it. Don't squander the gold of your days… Live the wonderful life that is in you!…Be always seeking new sensations. Be afraid of nothing… A new Hedonism – that is what our century wants. You might be its visible symbol…there is nothing you could not do. The world belongs to you for a season… The moment I met you I saw that you were quite unconscious of what you really are, of what you really might be. There was so much in you that charmed me…Youth! Youth! There is absolutely nothing in the world but youth!

John Gray may have been the inspiration for Dorian Gray the protagonist: the novel's prose was often both a manifesto of Wilde's middle years and a prefiguration of his affair with Lord Alfred Douglas.

LEFT: *'A Recollection' of the Café Royal by Max Beerbohm. The Café Royal was a well-known haunt of Wilde and his friends. Beerbohm's cartoon shows the artist Will Rothenstein (left) watching soberly as Wilde (right), Beerbohm and Charles Conder (centre) drink and carouse. 'Sober men,' recalled Rothenstein, 'are sorry companions for men crowned with vine leaves.'*

'Bosie' was a student at Wilde's *alma mater* Magdalen, also reading Greats, and editing a literary magazine, *Spirit Lamp*, when Wilde met him. He was the third son of the Marquess of Queensberry (author of the Queensberry rules for boxing), an eccentric aristocrat whose first wife, Bosie's mother, had divorced him for adultery. Queensberry was in turn domineering and protective of his offspring, attempting to moderate their behaviour by threatening to withhold their inheritance if it displeased him. He was, by his fiery, opinionated and often irrational nature, at odds with a lot of people a lot of the time.

In their passionate and consuming love affair, Wilde and Bosie were faithful in their fashion, but that fidelity allowed them to move together in two circles. One was a London social set of friends, families – according to Douglas, Constance Wilde 'liked me better than any of Oscar's other friends' – and acquaintances; the other comprised a number of homosexual relationships and casual encounters. Wilde periodically moved out of Tite Street and stayed in various London hotels in order to write, but also to entertain young men he had picked up or by whom he had been solicited. His intimacy with Douglas was intense, and at times tempestuous and peculiarly exhausting, since Bosie could be petulant, demanding and often violently angry.

'Dearest of all Boys,' Wilde wrote from the Savoy Hotel in March, 1893:

Your letter was delightful, red and yellow wine to me [It was Sherard who had delighted Wilde on their first acquaintance in Paris with the observation that white wine should properly be called yellow]; but I am sad and out of sorts. Bosie, you must not make scenes with me. They kill me, they wreck the loveliness of life. I cannot see you, so Greek and gracious, distorted with passion. I cannot listen to your curved lips saying hideous things to me. I would sooner be blackmailed by every renter [male prostitute] in London than have you bitter, unjust, hating. I must see you soon. You are the divine thing I want, the thing of grace and beauty...

RIGHT: *Max Beerbohm, caricatured by himself. Beerbohm was a schoolboy when he met Wilde, whom he referred to as 'the Divinity', predicting after reading* Salome *that 'if Oscar would rewrite all the Bible, there would be no sceptics'.*

The coloration of the love between Oscar Wilde and Lord Alfred Douglas, was, nevertheless, of passion and penury, the one in perpetual and restless dialogue with the other.

'I miss you so much,' Wilde wrote in April 1894, 'the gay, gilt and gracious lad has gone away – and I hate everyone else: they are tedious. Also I am in the purple valleys of despair, and no gold coins are dropping down from heaven to gladden me. London is very dangerous: writters come out at night and writ one, the roaring of creditors towards dawn is frightful, and solicitors are getting rabies and biting people.'

And in July Wilde wrote of friends who wanted him to accompany them to Paris:

ABOVE: *A haunting view from the fashionable Savoy hotel. Bosie and Wilde often stayed there. 'You begged me to take you to the Savoy,' Wilde later charged Bosie, 'that was indeed a visit fatal to me.' The hotel also had unhappy associations for Whistler, who stayed for three months with his terminally sick wife, Beatrice.*

…they say one wears flannels and straw hats and dines in the *Bois*, but, of course, I have no money, as usual, and can't go. Besides I want to see you. It is really absurd. *I can't live without you.* You are so dear, so wonderful. I think of you all day long, and miss your grace, your boyish beauty, the bright sword play of your wit, the delicate fancy of your genius, so surprising always in its sudden swallow-flights towards north and south, towards sun or moon – and, above all, you yourself…London is a desert without your dainty feet, and all the buttonholes have turned to weeds: Nettles and hemlock are 'the only wear'. Write me a line, and take all my love – now and for ever…

Despite his preoccupation with Bosie, and with money, by 1892 Wilde was beginning to write material that would make him famous and should have made him rich. As a brilliant – 'magical' in Bosie's words – conversationalist,

LEFT: *A photograph of Oscar Wilde and Lord Alfred Douglas in Oxford, c.1893. Wilde was later to write to Bosie: 'There is, I know, one answer to all that I have said to you, and that is that you loved me: that all through those two and a half years during which the fates were weaving into one scarlet pattern the threads of our divided lives you really loved me...'*

RIGHT: *A photograph of actors in* Lady Windermere's Fan, *in performance at St James's Theatre, 1892. The play provided a vehicle for several barbed Wildean truths: 'Do you know, I am afraid that good people do a great deal of harm in the world...It is absurd to divide people into good and bad. People are either charming or tedious. I take the side of the charming...'*

BELOW: *A sketch of George Alexander, actor/manager of the St James's Theatre, in the part of Lord Windermere.* Punch *was able to pun that Alexander was 'running Wilde' at the theatre.*

MR GEORGE ALEXANDER.

Wilde, the inveterate theatre-goer, had begun to turn again to play writing. He had had previous disappointments both with *Vera* and *The Duchess of Padua* (a five-act tragedy in blank verse in the style of Webster's *Duchess of Malfi*). *The Duchess of Padua* was finally staged in New York in January 1891 with a new title, *Guido Ferranti,* and with Wilde's name left off the credits. It was praised as being 'deft' but 'insincere', and 'less a tragedy than a melodrama'. When the impresario George Alexander took over the management of the St James's Theatre in London, Wilde responded to his request for a play by submitting the *Duchess.* Alexander declined it, but commissioned Wilde to write a contemporary play. The result – after a considerable delay – was *Lady Windermere's Fan* which Alexander thought was 'simply wonderful', offering Wilde £1,000 for the rights. Wilde turned Alexander's enthusiasm to his own advantage, 'A thousand pounds! I have so much confidence in your excellent judgement, my dear Alec, that I cannot but refuse your generous offer – I will take a percentage.' As a result of his acumen, Wilde made £7 000 in the first year of the play's production.

AUBREY BEARDSLEY

Wilde attended many of the rehearsals and argued with Alexander about various dramatic effects in his work, particularly over 'the element of suspense and curiosity, a quality so essentially dramatic'. In the play, which was subtitled 'A Play about a Good Woman', the repartee and smart society setting highlight hypocrisy as well as wit and the nature of goodness; the 'good' woman threatens to behave very 'badly,' and the 'bad' woman is in fact acting from the finest of motives.

Wilde sent out tickets for the opening night. Constance was in the audience, as was Mrs Bram Stoker (the former Florence Balcombe) and Lillie Langtry. Frank Harris, editor of the *Fortnightly Review*, 'had a box the first night and thinking it might do Oscar some good, I took with me Arthur Walter of *The Times*.' Robert Ross came sporting a green carnation, which Wilde had asked him to buy at a florist in the Burlington Arcade. Also present was a clerk from publishers the Bodley Head, Edward Shelley, whom it was alleged that Wilde bedded that night at the Albemarle Hotel.

Walter thought that 'the play was poor'; another critic found the 'humour is mechanical, unreal', but Harris was staunch, realizing that 'nine critics out of ten are incapable of judging original work'. He maintained that it was 'surely the best comedy in English, the most brilliant... I can compare it to the best of Congreve, and I think it's better.' Harris was confirmed in his view by the audience, 'the best heads in London, far superior in brains therefore to the average journalist, and their judgement was that it was a most brilliant and interesting play...Oscar Wilde had at last come into his kingdom.'

Lady Wilde had advised her younger son 'Do try to be *present yourself* at the *first performance*. It would be right and proper and Constance would like it', and, as the final curtain fell, the author strolled on stage – also wearing a green carnation. 'The house rose at him and cheered and cheered again' as Wilde, smoking a cigarette, which infuriated Henry James who was also in the audience, acknowledged the accolades with what he later described as 'a delightful and immortal speech':

LEFT: *'Love is easily killed. Oh! how easily love is killed.' A sketch by Aubrey Beardsley of the actress Winifred Emery, who played Mrs Erlynne in* Lady Windermere's Fan.

OSCAR WILDE

Ladies and Gentlemen: I have enjoyed this evening *immensely*. The actors have given us a *charming* rendering of a *delightful* play, and your appreciation has been *most* intelligent. I congratulate you on the *great* success of your performance, which persuades me that you think *almost* as highly of the play as I do myself.

The audience's role – or at least that of the men – had been to sport a green carnation in their lapels. These *verdigris* blooms, which were transformed by having dye injected, were the aesthete's flower, being a symbolic triumph of 'art over nature'. 'I want a good many men to wear them,' Wilde had instructed his friend, the artist and writer Graham Robertson, 'it will annoy the public…A young man on the stage will wear a green carnation; people will stare at it and wonder. Then they will look round the house and see every here and there more and more little specks of green. "This must be some secret symbol," they will say. "What on earth can it mean?" 'What does it mean?' asked Robertson. 'Nothing whatever,' said Wilde, 'but that is what nobody will guess.' However, Wilde knew well that in Paris a green carnation was the emblem of same-sex love.

Wilde then went on to supper with 'a small number of personal friends', (including Robert Ross, Reggie Turner and Bosie), whilst Constance, who 'looked charming in her pale brocaded gown', went home alone.

The Prince of Wales took a box; the play ran for 156 performances and went on tour in the provinces. Speranza, who had assured Oscar that she believed in 'you and your genius', found that she was kept so busy collecting and sending all the notices to Willie that she had hardly time to advise her son that now he had 'made your name and taken a distinguished place in the circle of intellects', he must also 'take care of yourself and of your health and keep clear of suppers and late hours and champagne.'

Within months of the success of *Lady Windermere's Fan* Oscar Wilde suffered an intense frustration. The play he had finished in Paris in November 1891 was written in French, for Wilde had intended that Sarah Bernhardt

LEFT: *'I must now pose as "the Mother of Oscar",' wrote Speranza to her son when* Lady Windermere's Fan *received such acclaim. 'To my dear, wonderful Mother,' he inscribed her copy of the play. This malicious sketch of the middle-aged, widowed Lady Wilde by Harry Furniss, depicts the ageing hostess as 'A walking mausoleum in gaudy jewels'.*

FANCY PORTRAIT.

QUITE TOO-TOO PUFFICKLY PRECIOUS!!

*Being Lady Windy-mère's Fan-cy Portrait of the new dramatic author,
Shakspeare Sheridan Oscar Puff, Esq.*

["He addressed from the stage a public audience, mostly composed of ladies,
pressing between his daintily-gloved fingers a still burning and half-smoked
cigarette."—*Daily Telegraph.*]

ABOVE: *The cover and inside
details of the programme for the first night
of* Lady Windermere's Fan *on 20
February 1892.*

LEFT: *A cartoon from* Punch, *5 March
1892, lampooning Wilde's behaviour as he
took a the curtain call on the opening
night of* Lady Windermere's Fan. *Wilde
exuberantly informed the audience: 'I must
tell you I think my piece excellent. And all
the puppets that have performed in it have
played extremely well. I hope you like my
piece as well as I do myself'.*

ABOVE: *The actress Sarah Bernhardt, in a woodcut by Sir William Nicholson, 1899. 'The only person in the world who could act Salome is Sarah Bernhardt, that "serpent of the old Nile", older than the Pyramids,' wrote WIlde. He was delighted that she 'saw in my play such beauty that she was anxious to produce it, to take herself the part of the heroine, to lend the entire poem of her personality …to my prose' although the production was never to take place.*

should play the part of Salome. Although, as he told her, Salome was not the star – the star was the moon. Ricketts was to be commissioned to do the stage design and Graham Robertson to design the costumes. It was to be an extravaganza of effects, posing intriguing dilemmas – should Salome be dressed as black night or a silver moon? Or green like a poisonous lizard? Or in gold with a breastplate of jewels? And could she be allowed to sport blue hair? Would Bernhardt (now aged forty-eight) dance the dance of the seven veils herself, or would a stand-in be prudent? These vexed questions and the rehearsals which had started in early June 1892 were abruptly halted later that month when the Lord Chamberlain's office intervened to ban the production of *Salome* on the British stage on the grounds that it depicted biblical characters. Wilde was incensed:

> If the Censor refuses *Salome*, I shall leave England and settle in France where I shall take out naturalisation. I will not consent to call myself a citizen of a country that shows such narrowness in artistic judgement. I am not English. I am Irish which is quite another thing.

But this was not to be the occasion that Wilde was to flee into exile, disgusted at the prurience and hypocrisy of the English.

Salome was, however, allowed to be published in book form. And in February 1893 a limited edition, bound in 'Tyrian purple [to suit the 'very gilt-haired' Bosie] and tired silver', appeared; it was described by *The Times* as 'an arrangement in blood and ferocity, morbid, *bizarre*, repulsive, and very offensive in its adaptation of scriptural phraseology to situations the reverse of sacred.'

The previous summer Wilde had written another play at the request of Sir Beerbohm Tree, half-brother of Max Beerbohm, who was the principal actor and also the manager of the Theatre Royal, Haymarket.

Wilde had rented a house at Babbacombe, near Torquay, from a kinswomen of Constance from mid-November 1892, for three months. 'I find the peace and beauty here so good for troubled nerves,' he wrote. For

RIGHT: *'The Eyes of Herod', an illustration by Aubrey Beardsley for* Salome, *published by Elkin Mathews and John Lane in 1894. As Beardsley conflated desires in his illustrations for* Salome, *so he transposed the now bloated Wilde into the lascivious Tetrarch. The symbols of Whistler, the butterfly and the peacock, are also present. Wilde thought the drawings 'quite wonderful', but had hoped for something more 'mystical', closer to the artist Gustave Moreau's décadent vision.*

RIGHT: *The programme for* A Woman of No Importance, *which opened at the Theatre Royal, Haymarket, on 19 April 1893. Wilde sent a ticket for the first night to the designer Graham Robertson, observing 'the rush for seats has been so enormous that we have had to refuse Royalties and bigwigs.'*

Theatre Royal   **Haymarket.**

Sole Lessee and Manager ... Mr. HERBERT BEERBOHM TREE

TO-NIGHT at 8.30,

A New and Original Play of Modern Life, entitled

A Woman of No Importance,

By OSCAR WILDE.

Lord Illingworth	...	Mr. TREE
Sir John Pontefract	...	Mr. HOLMAN CLARK
Lord Alfred Rufford ...	...	Mr. LAWFORD
Mr. Kelvil, M.P.	...	Mr. ALLAN
The Ven. James Daubeny, D.D. (Rector of Wrockley)	...	Mr. KEMBLE
Gerald Arbuthnot	...	Mr. FRED TERRY
Farquhar ... (Butler)	...	Mr. HAY
Francis ... (Footman)	...	Mr. MONTAGU
Lady Hunstanton	...	Miss ROSE LECLERCQ
Lady Caroline Pontefract ...	...	Miss LE THIÉRE
Lady Stutfield	...	Miss HORLOCK
Mrs. Allonby ...	...	Mrs. TREE
Hester Worsley	...	Miss JULIA NEILSON
Alice ... (Maid)	...	Miss KELLY
Mrs. Arbuthnot	...	Mrs. BERNARD BEERE

Printed for the Edwardes Menu Company, Limited, 6, Adam Street, A

[handwritten: 20th May 1893]

a time he was there *en famille*, and remained by the sea with his sons whilst Constance visited Italy and Bosie came to visit. Wilde explained the domestic *ménage* to Lady Mount-Temple: 'Indeed, Babbacombe Cliff has become a kind of college or school, for Cyril studies French in the nursery, and I write my new play in Wonderland [Lady Mount-Temple's boudoir], and in the drawing-room Lord Alfred Douglas – one of Lady Queensberry's sons – studies Plato with his tutor for his degree at Oxford in June. He and his tutor are staying with me for a few days, so I am not lonely.' However, in a letter to the tutor, Campbell Dodgson, who had returned to London, Wilde was to paint a rather more provocative and sexually charged reminiscence of those seaside days:

'I BECAME THE SPENDTHRIFT OF MY OWN GENIUS'

I am still conducting the establishment on the old lines and really think I have succeeded in combining the advantages of a public school with those of a private lunatic asylum, which you know, was my aim…

BABBACOMBE SCHOOL
Headmaster – Mr Oscar Wilde
Second Master – Mr Campbell Dodgson
Boys – Lord Alfred Douglas

Rules.
Tea for masters and boys at 9.30 a.m.
Breakfast at 10.30.
Work 11.30-12.30
At 12.30 Sherry and biscuits for headmaster and boys
(the second master objects to this).
12.40-1.30 Work.
1.30 Lunch.
2.30 4.30. Compulsory hide-and-seek for headmaster.
5. Tea for headmaster and second master,
brandy and sodas (not to exceed seven) for boys.
6-7. Work.
7.30. Dinner with compulsory champagne.
8.30-12. Ecarté, limited to five-guinea points.
12-1.30. Compulsory reading in bed. Any boy found disobeying this rule will be immediately woken up.

And the 'second master' himself wrote to the poet, Lionel Johnson:

Our life is lazy and luxurious; our moral principles are lax. We argue for hours in favour of different interpretations of Platonism. Oscar implores me, with outspread arms and tears in his eyes, to let my soul alone and cultivate my body for six weeks. Bosie is beautiful and fascinating, but quite wicked…we do no logic, no history, but play with pigeons and children and drive by the sea.

LEFT: The Damsel of the Sanct Grail by Dante Gabriel Rossetti, 1874. Wilde was enchanted by the pre-Raphaelite paintings in Lady Mount-Temple's house at Babbacombe. 'There are Rossetti drawings, and a window by Burne-Jones, and many lovely things and colours. I hear London like some grey monster raging over the publication of Salome, but I am at peace for the moment; all I desire is that the wind would cry like a thing whose heart is broken.'

Oscar sits…and meditates on his next play. I think him perfectly delightful with the firmest conviction that his morals are detestable…His command of language is extraordinary, so at least it seems to me who am inarticulate, and worship Irishmen who are not. I am going back on Saturday. I shall probably leave all that remains of my religion and morals behind me.

Rehearsals for the 'next play' started in March 1893, with Tree this time in the part of Lord Illingworth. Wilde again proved to be a constant presence at rehearsals – so much so that Tree was later to complain that he had produced the play not with the help, but 'with the interference of Wilde'.

A Woman of No Importance was again a story of concealment and revelation – this time a father, Lord Illingworth, discovers his long-lost illegitimate son, Gerald Arbuthnot. 'It is a woman's play,' Wilde wrote to an actor who

RIGHT: *'He is your father…' A sketch showing the dramatic disclosure from the first production of* A Woman of No Importance. *(subtitled 'A New and Original Play of Modern Life'). Beerbohm Tree played Lord Illingworth and Mrs Bernard Beere took the role of Mrs Arbuthnot.*

importuned him for a part, and it was the women who had the good lines. 'Lady Belton eloped with Lord Fethersall...Poor Lord Belton died three days afterwards of joy, or gout. I forget which,' says Lady Hunstanton, whilst another female character explains that women have a better time in life than men since 'there are far more things forbidden to us than are forbidden to them'.

A Woman of No Importance opened at St James's Theatre on 19 April 1893. This time Oscar Wilde did not address the audience after the final curtain. Looking 'very sweet in a new white waistcoat and a large bunch of lilies in his coat' (according to Max Beerbohm), he stood up in his box, declaring before an audience that included A.J.Balfour and Joseph Chamberlain, 'Ladies and gentlemen, I regret to inform you that Mr Oscar Wilde is not in the house', before taking his bow. The play ran for 118 nights. It made its author £100 a week. The critics were divided, but Wilde was happy. 'I shall always regard you as the best critic of my plays,' he told Beerbohm Tree in his dressing room after the first performance. 'But I have never criticised your plays,' responded the actor/manager. 'That is why,' retorted Wilde. And Speranza was her usual loyal and ecstatic self. 'You had a brilliant success,' she wrote, 'and I am so happy...I had a crowd here on Saturday evening; many had seen the play and nothing else was talked of...You are now a great sensation in London.'

LEFT: *Beardsley's frontispiece to the plays of John Davidson, published by John Lane in 1894, shows personalities of the London literary world. From left to right: Isabel Beardsley (an actress), Henry Harland, literary editor of* The Yellow Book, *Oscar Wilde, with vine leaves in his hair, Sir Augustus Harris, the poet, Richard Le Gallienne and Adeline Genée, a dancer.*

WHOSE PALLID BURDEN, SICK WITH PAIN, WATCHES THE WORLD WITH WEARIED EYES, AND WEEPS FOR EVERY SOUL THAT DIES, AND WEEPS FOR EVERY SOUL IN VAIN.

ABOVE and RIGHT: *Illustrations from 'The Sphinx', drawn by Charles Ricketts. The poem was published in 1894 by Matthews and Lane, in a limited edition of 250. Wilde had worked on the poem since his Oxford days, and he reprimanded Lane 'the maker of a poem is a "poet", not an "author".'*

Quite how much of a sensation Wilde was soon to make, no one could suspect, though the portents were there. At a party after the opening of *A Woman of No Importance* he had been distressed by a palmist who had suggested that his right palm indicated that he would 'send himself into exile'. Bosie and he were quarrelling. Bosie had come down from Oxford without taking a degree, a situation that did not please his parents, and he and Oscar spent part of the summer in a house on the river at Goring, where Douglas was supposed to be working on a translation of *Salome* and Wilde writing his next play. It seemed in one aspect idyllic: 'the river gods have lured me to devote myself to a Canadian canoe, in which I paddle about. It is shaped like a flower,' wrote Wilde but he also complained to Charles Ricketts, 'I have done no work here.' He found 'that life in a meadow and stream is far more complex than is life in streets and salons.' Later he was to recall to Bosie that at Goring:

you made a scene so dreadful, so distressing that I told you that we must part. I remember quite well, as we stood on the level croquet-ground with the pretty lawn all around us, that we were spoiling each other's lives, that you were absolutely ruining mine and that I evidently was not making you really happy, and that an irrevocable parting, a complete separation was the one wise philosophic thing to do. You went sullenly after luncheon, leaving one of your most offensive letters behind with the butler to be handed to me after your departure. Before three days had elapsed you were telegraphing from London to beg to be forgiven and allowed to return…I was always terribly sorry for the hideous temper to which you were really a prey. I was fond of you. So I let you come back and forgave you.

The 'wings of vulture creditors' were also circling around Wilde, and much of his desire to be free from the demanding presence of his lover was that he 'required rest and freedom from the terrible strain of your companionship. It was necessary for me to be a little by myself. It was intellectually necessary.' It was not only necessary for Wilde's artistic reputation, but also

RIGHT: *A playbill advertising* An Ideal Husband, *which opened at the Theatre Royal, Haymarket, on 3 January 1895. 'Do you consider* An Ideal Husband *[a play that portentously dealt with blackmail] the best of your plays?' a journalist from the* St James' Gazette *asked Wilde. 'They form a perfect cycle, and in their delicate sphere complete both life and art,' replied the satisfied author.*

ABOVE: *The part of Lady Chiltern in* An Ideal Husband *was taken by Julia Neilson. Wilde assured her husband that the 'part of Lady Chiltern is the important part, and the only sympathetic part...on her much of the fortune of the play will depend.' Lewis Waller, who was managing the theatre in Tree's absence, played Lord Chiltern; Charles Hawtry took the part of Lord Goring.*

essential for his financial solvency. He had taken rooms away from Tite Street in order to work on his next play:

> ...that first week you kept away...In that first week I wrote and completed in every detail, as it was ultimately performed, the first act of *An Ideal Husband*. The second week you returned and my work practically had to be given up. I arrived at St James's Place every morning at 11.30, in order to have the opportunity of thinking and writing without the interruptions inseparable from my own household, quiet and peaceful as that household was. But the attempt was vain. At twelve o'clock you drove up, and stayed smoking cigarettes and chattering until 1.30, when I had to take you out to luncheon at the Café Royal or the Berkeley. Luncheon with its *liqueurs* lasted usually till 3.30. For an hour you retired to White's. At teatime you appeared again, and stayed until it was time to dress for dinner. You dined with me either at the Savoy or at Tite Street. We did not separate as a rule till after midnight, as a supper at Willis' had to wind up the entrancing day. That was my life for those three months, every single day, except during the four days when you went abroad. I then, of course, had to go over to Calais to fetch you back. For one of my nature and temperament it was a position at once grotesque and tragic.

It was a relief to Wilde when Lady Queensberry took the advice he had offered her, sending Bosie 'abroad for four or five months, to the Cromers in Egypt if that could be managed'. Douglas left for Cairo at the end of that year. In the ensuing calm Wilde 'collected again the torn and ravelled web of my imagination, got my life back into my own hands, and not merely finished the three remaining acts of *An Ideal Husband*, but conceived and had almost completed two other plays of a completely different type, *A Florentine Tragedy* and *La Sainte Courtisane*...'

LEFT (above and below): *The cover and inside details from the programme for* An Ideal Husband. *Under Tree's management, the Theatre Royal, Haymarket became the smartest theatre in London...His audiences were as brilliant as his plays...the theatre was an aristocrat,' according to the theatre historian Maqueen-Pope. Wilde interfered constantly in rehearsals for his play, including calling one on Christmas Day. 'Don't you keep Christmas, Oscar?' chided Charles Brookfield, one of the actors. 'No...the only festival of the Church I keep is Septuagesima,' replied the playwright airily.*

RIGHT: *A caricature of George Bernard Shaw by Max Beerbohm, 1896. Shaw met Wilde in Dublin when both were young men, where 'we put each other out frightfully, and this odd difficulty persisted between us to the very last...' But Shaw was to write to Frank Harris on reading Harris' biography of Wilde: 'I understand why you say that you would rather have Wilde back than any friend you have ever talked to, even though he was incapable of friendship, though not without the most touching kindness on occasion.'*

An Ideal Husband opened at the Theatre Royal on 3 January 1895, with the Prince of Wales applauding from a box. Bernard Shaw acclaimed his fellow Irishman:

> Mr Wilde's new play at the Haymarket is a dangerous subject, because he has the property of making his critics dull. They laugh angrily at his epigrams, like a child who is being coaxed into being amused in the very act of setting up a yell of rage and agony. They protest that the trick is obvious, and that such epigrams can be turned out by the score by anyone light-minded enough to condescend to such frivolity. As far as I can ascertain, I am the only person in London who cannot sit down and write an Oscar Wilde play at will. The fact that his plays, though apparently lucrative, remain unique under these circumstances, says much for the self-denial of our scribes. In a certain sense Mr Wilde is to me our only thorough playwright. He plays with everything: with wit, with philosophy, with drama, with actors and audiences, with the whole theatre.

In August 1894 Wilde embarked upon the play that is his vehicle of fame. 'I send you the first copy of my somewhat farcical comedy [which he was reputed to have written in three weeks],' Wilde wrote to George Alexander at the end of October 1894. 'It is called *Lady Lancing* on the cover: but the real title is *The Importance of Being Earnest*. When you read the play, you will see the punning title's meaning.'

Wilde explained that the play 'was exquisitely trivial, a delicate bubble of fantasy, and it has its philosophy...that we should treat all the trivial things of life very seriously, and all the serious things of life with sincere and studied triviality...realism is only a background; it cannot form an artistic motive for a play that is to be a work of art.' But in life realism was coming ominously to the foreground.

Wilde and Bosie had been reconciled by the end of March 1894 – not without misgivings on Wilde's side. He was later to recognize: 'My fault was not that I did not part from you, but that I parted from you far too often...'

George Bernard Shaw Esq

RIGHT: *The* Yellow Book *has appeared. It is dull and loathsome, a great failure. I am so glad,'* Wilde wrote to Bosie. *Nevertheless the* Yellow Book, *which first appeared in April 1894, has enjoyed a* succès de scandale *ever since as the epitome of the decadent* fin de siècle. *Aubrey Beardsley was its art editor, but he was continually required by the publisher, John Lane, to redraw his sexually explicit covers. Beardsley was dismissed after volume IV appeared and 'the yellow book turned to grey overnight'. Wilde was not invited to contribute to the journal, but its reputation was such that it was widely, and inaccurately, reported that Wilde was carrying the* Yellow Book *when he was arrested. In fact it was a copy of Pierre Louÿs' novel,* Aphrodite, *also bound in yellow.*

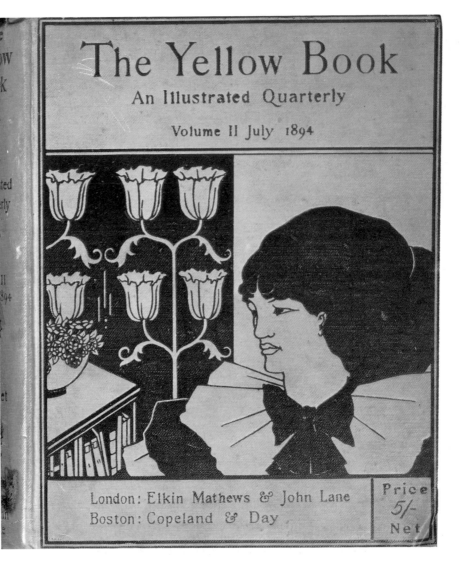

ABOVE: *Aubrey Beardsley, caricatured by Max Beerbohm in April 1896. For Wilde, Beardsley 'brought a strange new personality to English art'.*

RIGHT: *Aubrey Beardsley, painted by Walter Sickert in 1894, at the unveiling of a bust to Keats in Hampstead church. The young Beardsley recognized 'I shall not live longer than did Keats.' He died of consumption on 16 March 1898, aged 25; Wilde lamented that 'one who added another terror to life should have died at the age of a flower'.*

'I am passionately fond of him and he of me,' Bosie had written to his mother while he was in Egypt. 'There is nothing I would not do for him and if he dies before I do I shall not care to live any longer. Surely there is nothing but what is fine and beautiful in such a love as that of two people for one another, the love of the disciple and the philosopher.'

However, Wilde had resolved to take the opportunity of Bosie's absence to try yet again to end his 'fatal friendship' with him. The disciple had written daily from his travels, but the philosopher had resolutely left his letters unanswered. In desperation Bosie even enlisted the help of Constance to intercede: Wilde remained implacable. 'Time heals every wound but for many months to come I will neither write to you nor see you,' he telegraphed to Douglas in March 1894. Bosie fired off an eleven-page telegram entreating Wilde to join him in Paris, and hinting that he could not be responsible for the consequences if Wilde continued to deny him his love.

Wilde relented: 'When I arrived in Paris,' he wrote, 'your tears breaking out again and again all through the evening, and falling over your cheeks like rain as we sat, at dinner first at Voisin's, at supper at Paillard's afterwards: the unfeigned joy you evinced at seeing me, holding my hand whenever you could, as though you were a gentle and penitent child: your contrition, so simple, so sincere, at that moment; made me consent to renew our friendship.'

One crisis rapidly followed another, as events began to assume their own momentum. Wilde was to remember them in hideous detail. 'Two days after we had returned to London [Wilde having spent £150 in Paris, including £85 in restaurants], your father saw you having luncheon with me at the Café Royal, joined my table, drank of my wine, and that afternoon, through a letter addressed to you, began his first attack on me.'

Alfred…Your intimacy with this man Wilde…must either cease or I will disown you and stop all money supplies. I am not going to try and analyse this intimacy, and I make no charge; but to my mind to pose as a thing is as

bad as to be it. With my own eyes I saw you both in the most loathsome and disgusting relationship as expressed by your manner and expression. no wonder people are talking as they are...I hear on good authority...that his wife is petitioning to divorce him for sodomy and other crimes...If I thought the actual thing was true, and it had become public property, I should be quite justified in shooting him at sight.

> Your disgusted so-called father, Queensberry.

Bosie's reply was pugilistic: 'What a funny little man you are' he telegraphed on 2 April 1894. 'You impertinent young jackanapes,' shot back Queensberry, 'I request that you will not send such messages...if you send me any more such telegrams or come with any impertinence, I will give you the thrashing you deserve...If I catch you again with that man I will make a public scandal in a way you little dream of.'

Wilde was aghast by Bosie's action ('a telegram of which the commonest street-boy would have been ashamed') and forced to recognize:

I know that you really loved me [but] in you Hate was always stronger than Love. Your hatred of your father was of such stature that it entirely outstripped, o'erthrew, and overshadowed your love of me...to gratify it you gambled with my life, as you gambled with my money, carelessly, recklessly, indifferent to the consequences...When your father first began to attack me it was as your private friend, and in a private letter to you...I saw at once that a terrible danger was looming on the horizon of my troubled days: I told you I would not be a catspaw between you both in your ancient hatred of each other.

At the end of June 1894 Queensberry called on Wilde at home. 'In my library at Tite Street, waving his small hands in the air in epileptic fury, your father ...had stood uttering every foul word his foul mind could think of, and screaming the loathsome threats he afterwards with such cunning carried out.' Queensberry went 'from restaurant to restaurant looking for me, in order to insult me before the whole world, and in such a manner

LEFT: A caricature of Wilde as a pig by Beatrice Whistler, the wife of James McNeill Whistler. Herself an artist, she designed jewellery and decorative panels for furniture; she also worked with Whistler on life drawings and small portraits. Her first husband, the architect E.W. Godwin, had been responsible for the transformation of both Whistler's and Wilde's houses in Tite Street.

that if I retaliated I would be ruined, and if I did not retaliate I would be ruined also.'

If Wilde felt hunted, Bosie seems to have had the smell of the chase in his nostrils and defiantly informed his father, 'Ever since your exhibition at O.W's house, I have made a point of appearing with him at many public restaurants such as The Berkeley, Willis's Rooms and the Café Royal etc, and shall continue to go to any of these places whenever I choose and with whom I choose.' As Oscar was to write from prison 'The prospect of battle in which you would be safe delighted you. I never remember you in higher spirits than you were for the rest of the season.'

By early 1895, Wilde was about to launch a third audaciously amusing production on the West End; *The Importance of Being Earnest* was scheduled to open on St Valentine's Day, 14 February 1895. Wilde was on the cusp of his greatest public success. But as he wrote against the grain of Victorian society pretentions, so he lived against it too: he was reckless in his life as in his writing. He had once explained to a journalist why he felt so drawn to Paris: 'While one is in London one hides everything; in Paris one reveals everything.' However, it was clear that in fact Wilde was hiding very little.

On 17 January, Wilde wrote to Ada Leverson 'I fly to Algiers with Bosie tomorrow. I begged him to let me stay to rehearse, but so beautiful is his nature that he declined at once.' In Algiers, where Wilde and Bosie had gone to find boys in the casbah, they unexpectedly met Gide again. Fearful of himself, as of them, Gide nearly fled after seeing their names inscribed in the hotel register; he wrote to his mother that Wilde was 'the most dangerous product of civilisation…on the London and Paris black-lists' and he and Bosie were 'the most compromising people in the

LEFT: *'Oscar's Valentine', a cartoon satirizing the dual romances of* The Importance of Being Earnest *which opened on 14 February 1895 at the Theatre Royal, Haymarket. Algernon: 'I hope, Cecily, I shall not offend you if I state quite frankly and openly that you seem to me to be in every way the visible personification of absolute perfection.' Cecily: 'I think your frankness does you great credit, Ernest. If you will allow me, I will copy your remarks into my diary… it is only a very young girl's thoughts and impressions and consequently meant for publication'.*

world'. He was aghast at the news of Queensberry's pursuit 'But if you go back, what will happen? Do you realise the risk?' But Wilde was trapped – by his nature. 'My friends advise me to be prudent. Prudent! How could I be that? It would mean going backwards. I must go as far as possible. I cannot go any further…'

It was not only Bosie's taunts that goaded Queensberry. First in September 1894 a thinly veiled parody of Wilde's relationship with his son had appeared in the form of *The Green Carnation* written by Robert Hichens. Wilde considered it 'a middle-class and mediocre book' that usurped the strangely beautiful name of the green carnation (which Wilde acknowledged he invented). Queensberry read the book and understood its references to 'Mr Amarinth' and 'Lord Reggie'. On 18 October his eldest and favourite son, Viscount Drumlanrig, had been found dead, with all the appearance of suicide resulting from the threat of blackmail over his homosexual relations with the Secretary of State for Foreign Affairs, Lord Rosebery. Two days later Queensberry had received the final decree of the contested annulment of his second marriage. (The second Lady Queensberry had left her husband immediately after their wedding on 1 November 1893, seeking an annulment on the grounds of alleged 'malformation of the parts of generation' coupled with 'frigidity and impotence'.)

On the eve of the opening of *The Importance of Being Earnest,* Wilde got wind of Queensberry's intention to be present at the first night. He wrote to the business manager of the St James's Theatre, 'Lord Queensberry is at Carter's Hotel, Albemarle Street. Write to him from Mr Alexander that you regret to find that the seat given to him was already sold, and return him his money. This will prevent trouble, I hope.' It didn't. Three days later

LEFT: *André Gide, photographed in Biskra, Algeria, in 1895. 'You listen with your eyes,' Wilde had flattered Gide when they first met in Paris. In January 1895 Wilde and Bosie met him again whilst they were on holiday in Algiers. Gide recalled: 'Wilde had certainly changed. One felt less softness in his look, something raucous in his laughter and something frenzied in his joy. He seemed both more sure of pleasing and less ambitious to succeed in doing so…He would walk in the streets of Algiers, preceded, escorted, followed by an extraordinary band of ragamuffins…he recognised them all with joy and tossed money to them haphazardly.'*

RIGHT: On the Road to Biskra *by Emile Friant. 'There is a great deal of beauty here,' wrote Wilde to Robert Ross. 'The Kabyle boys are quite lovely. At first we had some difficulty in procuring a proper civilised guide. But now it is all right, and Bosie and I have taken to hashish: it is quite exquisite. three puffs of smoke and then peace and love. The beggars here have profiles, so the problem of poverty is easily solved.' Bosie was to follow one of the 'quite lovely' boys along the road to Biskra: Wilde had to return to London alone for the final rehearsals of* The Importance of Being Earnest.

OSCAR WILDE

Greek days.' This letter might 'appear extravagant to those in the habit of writing commercial correspondence,' Clarke conceded, but his client was a poet who had written a 'prose sonnet' of which he was entirely unashamed and could not be judged by the hateful and repulsive standards that Queensberry implied.

In the spring of that year Douglas had given one Alfred Wood a seventeen-year old boy whose sexual favours he and Wilde were sharing, one of his cast-off suits – without first checking through the pockets. Wood had found some letters from Wilde – including the above – and decided that they had potential for blackmail. Wood was anxious to get money to go to America. In April he had sent a copy of the 'Hyacinthus' letter to Beerbohm Tree who, at the time, was involved in the production of *A Woman of No Importance*. Beerbohm had warned Wilde and when Wood approached him claiming to have been offered £60 for the letter, Wilde was insouciant: 'If you take my advice,' he reported himself as having said, 'you will go to that man and sell my letter to him for £60. I myself have never received so large a sum for any prose work of that length; but I am glad to find that there is someone in England who considers a letter of mine worth £60.' Eventually Wilde claimed he had given Wood and two of his fellow scoundrels money to retrieve his letters to Bosie – minus the incriminating 'Hyacinthus' one. Wood had then gone to America, but was discovered back in London when Queensberry's lawyers were constructing their case.

When Edward Carson rose to cross-examine Wilde, he was careful to emphasise the sixteen-year age difference between Wilde – who was 'careless' about his age, and was, in fact, forty – and Douglas, aged twenty-four. Wilde treated his interrogation as an opportunity for elegant point scoring: when Carson quoted verse from one of Wilde's articles and said 'I suppose you wrote that also, Mr Wilde?' Wilde took a long time to answer. The court was expectant as he replied quietly 'Ah no, Mr Carson, Shakespeare wrote that.' When Carson suggested that 'the affection and love of the artist of Dorian Gray might lead an ordinary individual to

LEFT: *Edward Carson, the brilliant young barrister who had been a student with Wilde at Trinity College, Dublin, and was later to 'play the orange card' in the partition of Ireland. When Wilde heard that Carson had been engaged to represent the Marquess of Queensberry, he is alleged to have said with resignation: 'No doubt he will perform his task with the added bitterness of an old friend.' In fact, Carson deliberated for some time before accepting the brief.*

RIGHT: *Sir Edward Clarke, M.P., Q.C., who acted for Wilde. 'I can only accept this brief [to prosecute Queensberry for libel], Mr Wilde,' he warned, 'if you can assure me on your honour as an Engish gentleman that there is not and never has been any foundation for the charges that are made against you.' Wilde assured his counsel that the allegations that he was 'posing as a sodomite' were 'absolutely groundless.'*

believe that it might have a certain tendency,' Wilde's riposte was 'I have no knowledge of the views of ordinary individuals'. When Carson bluntly asked: 'Have you ever adored a young man madly?' Wilde replied languorously, 'No, not madly. I prefer love – that is a higher form…I have never given adoration to anybody except myself.'

Carson then embarked on a damaging list of 'homeless and shiftless boys' – Alfred Wood, William Allen, Robert Clibborn, Charles Parker, a valet, his brother, and a groom, Alfred Taylor, who were prepared to testify to their relationship with Wilde. The lawyers had been helped in their searches by the actor who had complained about rehearsing on Christmas Day, Charles Brookfield (Thackeray's illegitimate son) and another actor in Wilde's plays, Charles Hawtry, who had co-authored a parody on Wilde *The Poet and the Puppet*. A private detective had happened on a prostitute who complained that trade was bad – she was losing clients to boys mentored by Oscar Wilde. 'All you have to do is break into the top flat at 13 Little College Street, behind Westminster Abbey, and you will find all the evidence you require,' she volunteered. These were the lodgings of Alfred Taylor and Wilde was alleged to be a frequent visitor to the flat. There the eager detective found the names and addresses of Wilde's 'boys', lads living across London from Mayfair to the Mile End Road. Carson intoned yet more names – Fred Atkins, whom Wilde had taken to Paris, a servant at Bosie's rooms in Oxford, Walter Grainger, Sidney Mavor (known mainly as 'Jenny'), and Ernest Scarfe.

Again Wilde was insouciant, claiming there was nothing surprising in the fact that a self-proclaimed artist mixed with working boys of little education. 'I didn't care two pence what they were. I liked them. I have a passion to civilise the community.' Then there was Edward Shelley, 'the office boy' at Wilde's publishers, and Alfonso Harold Conway – 'did he not sell newspapers on the pier [at Worthing]?' questioned Carson, 'No,' said Wilde, 'it is the first I have heard of his connection with literature.' Carson persisted 'Did you take the lad to Brighton?' 'Yes.' 'And provide him with

a suit of blue serge?' 'Yes.' 'And a straw hat with a band of red and blue?' 'That, I think, was his unfortunate selection.' 'I recognise no social distinction of any kind,' Wilde loftily maintained as the register of working boys and unemployed young men unrolled, 'and to me youth, the mere fact of youth, is so wonderful that I would rather talk to a young man for half an hour than [he paused meaningfully] be cross examined in court.' However, it was not only talk that had to be explained away; there were gifts of silver cigarette cases, signed photographs, sums of money, smart restaurant meals, iced champagne, whisky and sodas, shared cabs – and shared hotel rooms. What did Wilde get from all this? The aesthete explained in answer to Carson's question that he did not kiss Grainger because 'he was a peculiarly plain boy…if I were asked why I did not kiss a door-mat, I should say I do not like to kiss door-mats.' It was one flippant response too many.

Wilde's counsel knew that the evidence was stacked against his client, and feared that worse was to come when Carson intimated that several of the boys mentioned were prepared to testify. The next morning Clarke admitted in court that what the jury had heard could well lead them to the conclusion that there was 'sufficient justification' for Queensberry's charge that Wilde was 'posing' as a sodomite, and that the prosecution was prepared to accept that the Marquess had some justification for his use of the word 'posing.' 'I trust,' Clarke concluded 'that this may make an end of the case.' But it was to be only the beginning.

THE TRIAL

WITHIN THE

CENTRAL CRIMINAL COURT,
OLD BAILEY, LONDON
WEDNESDAY, 3RD APRIL, 1895.

Judge—
THE HON. MR. JUSTICE COLLINS

Counsel for the Prosecution—

SIR EDWARD CLARKE, Q.C., M.P.
MR. CHARLES WILLIE MATHEWS.
MR. TRAVERS HUMPHREYS.
(Instructed by Messrs. C. O. Humphreys, Son, & Kershaw)

Counsel for the Defendant, the Marquess of Queensberry—

MR. EDWARD CARSON, Q.C., M.P.
MR. CHARLES FREDERICK GILL.
MR. ARTHUR GILL.
(Instructed by Messrs. Day, Russell & Company.)

Counsel for Lord Alfred Douglas and Lord Douglas of Hawick—

MR. EDWARD BESLEY, Q.C.
MR. JOHN LIONEL MONCKTON.
(Instructed by Messrs. C. O. Humphreys, Son, & Kershaw)
105

LEFT: *The court card with details of Wilde's prosecution of Queensberry in 1895. 'An English court of law gives me no assurance of a fair trial,' Frank Harris warned Wilde, 'or rather I am certain that in matters of art or morality an English court is about the worst tribunal in the civilised world…Don't forget that if you lose and Queensberry goes free, everyone will hold that you are guilty of nameless vice…You are sure to lose.' The expert opinion was that 'no English jury would give Oscar Wilde a verdict against anyone'.*

LEFT: *'It would have been impossible for me to have proved my case without putting Lord Alfred Douglas in the witness box against his father,'* Wilde wrote to the editor of the Evening News *on 5 April 1895. 'Lord Alfred Douglas was extremely anxious to go into the box, but I would not let him do so. Rather than put him in so painful a position I determined to retire from the case, and to bear on my own shoulders whatever ignominy and shame might result from my prosecuting Lord Queensberry.'*

CHAPTER 5

'I HAVE GOT AS FAR AS THE HOUSE OF DETENTION'

LEFT: *The Boulevard* from Quelques aspects de la vie de Paris *by Pierre Bonnard, 1899. On his release from prison in May 1897, Oscar Wilde settled for a time in Berneval-sur-Mer, claiming: 'If I live in Paris I may be doomed to things I don't desire. I am afraid of big towns.' Less than a year later, however, a letter to the publisher Leonard Smithers from Naples announced 'I shall be in Paris on Sunday next. It is my only chance of working. I miss an intellectual atmosphere, and I am tired of Greek bronzes...My life has gone to great ruin here, and I have no brains now, or energy. I hope to make an effort in Paris.'*

On 5 April 1895 the jury at the Old Bailey returned a verdict of 'not guilty' in the libel trial brought by Oscar Wilde against the Marquess of Queensberry. The verdict indicated that Queensberry had been justified in calling Wilde a sodomite in the public interest. The packed court room had cheered and the judge passed Queensberry's counsel, Edward Carson, a note congratulating him on his 'searching crossXam' and having 'escaped the rest of the filth'. Within minutes of the collapse of the case, the trial papers had been sent to the Director of Public Prosecutions.

The press almost universally crowed at the result:

> There is not a man or woman in the English-speaking world possessed of the treasure of a wholesome mind...not under a deep debt of gratitude to the Marquess of Queensberry for destroying the High Priest of the Decadents.

Wilde had again been given a chance to escape to France. According to Frank Harris, Wilde's lawyer would have kept the prosecution parade rolling if his client required time to flee abroad, otherwise, in the face of the mounting evidence it was pointless. However, Wilde elected not to flee despite the urgent and repeated pleadings of his friends that he should take the boat train for France (the warrant for his arrest was not issued until a quarter of an hour after its departure). It was later estimated that 600 other gentlemen crossed to Calais that night.

Whilst Bosie rushed to the House of Commons to seek help from one of his relatives, Wilde, Turner and Ross could do nothing but sit in the Cadogan Hotel in Sloane Street, waiting.

ABOVE: *Frank Harris caricatured by Beerbohm, 1896. Harris had strongly urged Wilde to flee rather than pursue the Queensberry libel case: 'you are a sort of standard bearer for future generations. If you lose you will make it harder for all writers in England... you will put the clocks back fifty years.'*

BITER BIT

ABOVE: *A sketch showing the arrest of Wilde from the* Police News. *The tension of waiting was over:*

> He sipped at a weak hock and seltzer
> As he gazed at the London skies...
> 'I want some more hock in my seltzer,
> And Robbie, please give me your hand—
> Is this the end or beginning?
> How can I understand?'

From The Arrest of Oscar Wilde at the Cadogan Hotel *by John Betjeman.*

At ten minutes past six in the evening of 5 April 1895, a waiter, accompanied by two police officers, knocked on the door of room 53. One of the detectives stepped into the room, saying 'We have a warrant here, Mr Wilde, for your arrest on a charge of committing indecent acts.' Wilde, who had gone 'very grey in the face', was then escorted in a cab to Bow Street Police Station.

Nearly every day before the trial opened, Bosie visited Wilde, first at Bow Street and then in Holloway Prison, where he was on remand. Unlike Ross, who had reluctantly gone to France, Bosie stayed during this dismal period, writing letters to the press declaring that judgement had been passed on Wilde before his trial opened. 'Nothing but Alfred Douglas's daily visits quicken me into life, and even him I only see under humiliating and tragic conditions.' Sitting opposite each other and separated by a corridor, Wilde's deafness in one ear and the interminable noise of other prisoners meant that he could hardly hear what Bosie said, and as the men tried to converse tears coursed down both their faces.

Wilde wrote from Holloway to Ada Leverson and her husband, Ernest, of the comfort that he nevertheless derived from these emotionally searing occasions:

> I write to you from prison, where your kind words have reached me and given me comfort, though they have made me cry in my loneliness. Not that I am really alone. A slim thing, gold-haired like an angel, stands always at my side. His presence overshadows me. He moves in the gloom like a white flower.

BELOW: *Holloway Prison, London, at that time a men's prison, where Wilde was remanded for a period between his trials. In the original version of* The Importance of Being Earnest, *Algernon is arrested for debt and objects vehemently to the prospect of detention in Holloway: 'Well, I really am not going to be imprisoned in the suburbs for having dined in the West End. It is perfectly ridiculous.'*

Finally, on the insistence of Wilde's lawyer, who felt that his presence would be detrimental to his client's interests in court by reminding the jury of the charge of corrupting an innocent youth, Bosie left for France. Wilde, he recalled, 'kissed the end of my finger through an iron grating at Newgate, and begged me to let nothing in the world alter my attitude and my conduct towards him.'

Those of Wilde's books still in print were withdrawn from sale; *An Ideal Husband*, playing at the Criterion, closed; Wilde's name was pasted over on the billboards for *The Importance of Being Earnest*, then it, too, closed. The bailiffs moved into Tite Street, to Wilde's anguish:

> ...all my charming things are to be sold: my Burne-Jones drawings; my Whistler drawings; my Monticelli; my Simeon Solomons; my china; my Library with its collection of presentation volumes from almost every poet of my time, from Hugo to Whitman, from Swinburne to Mallarmé, from Morris to Verlaine; with its beautifully bound editions of my father's and mother's works; its wonderful array of college and school prizes, its *éditions de luxe* at give away prices.

The trial of Oscar Wilde opened at the Old Bailey on 26 April 1895. He stood in the dock with Alfred Taylor, charged with twenty-five acts of gross indecency contrary to the Criminal Law Amendment Act of 1885, Section 11. It was the first time that 'indecent relations' between men in private had been designated a criminal offence; this was also the notorious Act which excluded lesbianism from its terms of reference, since it is alleged Queen Victoria firmly asserted that 'women would not do such things'. There was in addition a conspiracy to procure charge, which was subsequently dropped. Alfred Taylor was also charged with having acted as a procurer for Wilde. The charges related to the Parker brothers, Frederick Atkins, Sidney Mavor, the would-be blackmailer Alfred Wood and Edward Shelley (the Bodley Head clerk); and two further charges concerned incidents at the Savoy Hotel.

RIGHT: *A reconstruction of Wilde's progress from lecture hall to court room by the* Police News, *as Wilde's first trial reached its conclusion. 'Are you a dramatist and author?' Wilde was asked to establish at the committal proceedings at Great Marlborough Street on 9 March 1895. 'I believe I am well known in that capacity,' he replied, and received an immediate rebuke from the magistrate; 'Only answer the questions please.' For Wilde, the Old Bailey was inevitably another arena for performance and to his great detriment he played to the gallery on too many occasions.*

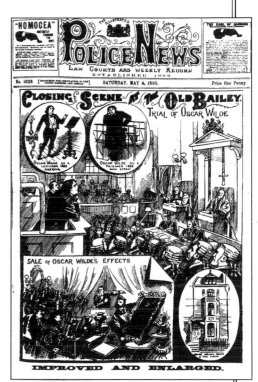

OSCAR WILDE

The strain of the last weeks had told on Wilde: it was noted that he looked thin, ill-kempt, anxious and tired as the trial rehearsed much of the same evidence as had been heard three weeks earlier at the libel hearing. This time the boys were there in person, however, to testify to dinners in restaurants with red-shaded candles, a generosity of champagne, brandies and coffee, cabs, liqueurs, hock and seltzers, cigarettes, gold rings, all paid for by Wilde; gifts of money, £3, £4, £30, £300, talk of poetry and art. There were descriptions of going into bedrooms in London hotels and lying on sofas in Tite Street; of kisses and protests, and then more kisses; of sitting on Wilde's lap 'imagining I was a girl and he was my lover; of being called 'Mrs Wilde' and 'Miss Oscar'; of cabs to the Savoy hotel; of more liqueurs; of the 'act of sodomy'. Landladies gave evidence of rooms where daylight was never admitted, lighted as they were by coloured candles, furnished with mattresses and strewn with women's wigs, shoes and stockings, and perfumed with women's scent, where it was 'always gentlemen' who called. Hotel staff were summoned by the prosecution to recall boys with sallow complexions in Wilde's bed, and sheets 'stained in a peculiar way.'

When Wilde took the stand he denied all charges of indecency, whilst admitting that he had 'taken up with these youths' since he was 'a lover of youth…I like to study the young in everything. There is something fascinating in youthfulness'. He agreed that he would probably 'prefer puppies to dogs and kittens to cats'. He conceded that he had visited Taylor's rooms 'to amuse myself sometimes; to smoke a cigarette; for music, chatting and nonsense of that kind, to while an hour away'. Asked if these rooms were not in 'rather a rough neighbourhood', Wilde demurred: 'that I don't know. I know it is near the Houses of Parliament.'

ABOVE: *A portrait of Oscar Wilde by Henri de Toulouse-Lautrec, 1895. The artist, who had sketched Wilde in Paris, was in London on the eve of his trial, and met Wilde, who was looking strained. Wilde refused to sit for a portrait, but on returning to his hotel room Toulouse-Lautrec made a sketch from memory, adding the Houses of Parliament as the location.*

ABOVE: *A sketch from the Savoy, a hotel which featured frequently in evidence at Wilde's various trials, by Whistler. 'I shall prove that Mr Wilde brought boys into the Savoy Hotel. The masseur of that establishment — a most respectable man — and other servants will be called to prove the character of Mr Wilde's relations with his visitors,' promised Sir Edward Carson at the trial of the Marquess of Queensberry for libel.*

RIGHT: At the Café Royal *by Sidney Starr, 1888. Wilde often dined with Bosie and other friends at the Café; it was also a venue for entertaining boys or 'feasting with panthers'. Frank Harris recalled how on one occasion he encountered Wilde there with two 'quite common' youths. 'He was talking as well as if he had had a picked audience...about the Olympic games, telling how the youths wrestled... and won the myrtle wreath ...nude, clothed only in sunshine and beauty.'*

LEFT: *A photograph of the marble statue of Hermes by the Greek sculptor Praxiteles. A cast of this celebrated work had stood in the corner of Wilde's study in Tite Street. In his work 'The Critic as Artist', Wilde had written of how 'the sculptor hewed from the marble block the great white-limbed Hermes that slept within it'. 'Why did you take up with these youths?' asked the prosecution at Wilde's trial. 'I am a lover of youth!' he replied. 'You exalt youth as some sort of god?' The ideal of Hellenic male beauty inspired the classical scholar and aesthete throughout his 'Art and Life'.*

But it was not all talk of 'renters' and 'pimps'. Wilde was also quizzed about his views on the morality of literature and its potential to corrupt, with particular reference to the poems of Lord Alfred Douglas. When Bosie's poem 'Two Loves' was read out, Wilde responded:

> The 'Love that dare not speak its name' in this century is such a great affection of an elder for a younger man as there was between David and Jonathan, such as Plato made the very basis of his philosophy, and such as you find in the sonnets of Michaelangelo and Shakespeare…It is that deep, spiritual affection that is as pure as it is perfect…It is in this century misunderstood, so much misunderstood that it may be described as the 'Love that dare not speak its name' and on account of it I am placed where I am now. It is beautiful, it is fine, it is the noblest form of affection. There is nothing unnatural about it. It is intellectual and it frequently exists between an elder and a younger man, when the elder man has intellect, and the younger man has all the joy, hope and glamour of life before him. That it should be so the world does not understand. The world mocks at it and sometimes puts one in the pillory for it.

The gallery 'burst into applause – I am sure it affected the jury,' noted Max Beerbohm, who recognized in the circumstances it was a magnificient achievement: 'He has never had so great a triumph'. Nevertheless, the jury could not agree about Wilde's alleged acts of indecency and a new trial was ordered.

Wilde was eventually allowed bail while awaiting trial; but the world outside at first seemed no more hospitable than his cell. No hotel was prepared to accept him as a guest. Bosie was holed up in the Hôtel de la Poste in Rouen, as was Ross. He was obliged to make an appeal to his estranged brother – 'Willie, give me shelter or I shall die in the streets' – and take refuge in Oakley Street, Chelsea. His mother was also living in the house with Willie and his second wife. It was another form of purgatory. 'Willie makes such merit of giving me shelter…it is all dreadful,' he told his

ABOVE: *The writer Ada Leverson (née Beddington) whom Wilde greatly admired and whom he named after the title of his own poem. 'You are the most wonderful Sphinx in the world.' When he was arrested and awaiting trial his admiration deepened. '[I] have no words to thank you for all that you do for me, but for you and Ernest [her husband] Bosie and I have deepest love …you are good and gentle and wonderful.'*

friend Frank Harris, who continued to urge him to flee with talk of 'a brougham and fast horse' and a 'little yacht moored at Erith…in one hour she would be free of the Thames and on the high seas…' Wilde again refused. However, he did accept the courageous invitation of his friend the 'Sphinx', Ada Leverson, and her husband Ernest to stay at their house in Kensington. Before the Sphinx had met Wilde, some years before, she had been told that he was 'like a giant with the wings of a Brazilian butterfly', and she was not disappointed. Now she was to compare him to 'a hunted stag', and offered him rooms on the nursery floor, where 'in the presence of a rocking horse, golliwogs, a blue and white nursery dado with rabbits and other animals on it, the most serious and tragic matters were discussed…with his solicitor.' The Leversons had called all the servants together before Wilde arrived. 'We told them who was coming, offering them a month's wages if they wished to leave at once.' The servants behaved better than most of Wilde's friends, as 'each…in turn refused to leave. They appeared proud to wait on "poor Mr Wilde" '. As a precaution, however, the Leversons 'sent the coachman away for a holiday, as we feared he might talk in public houses'.

Constance visited Wilde at the Leversons and left in tears when he refused the message she had brought from his lawyer urging him to flee. Ada sent him a note with the same plea. When Wilde appeared for dinner, he handed her back the note saying reproachfully 'That is not like you, Sphinx.' And then he began to talk of absinthe, of opium dens in Limehouse, of Baudelaire and Poe, of enjoyment and of books. And he uttered his memorable judgement on Dickens: 'One must have a heart of stone to read the death of Little Nell without laughing.'

On 20 May 1895 the second trial of Oscar Wilde opened. Ada Leverson had thought that he was 'generally extremely optimistic, firmly believing in a palmist's prophecy of triumph', but that morning he turned to her as he left for court and said 'for the first time in a faltering voice, "If the worst comes to the worst, Sphinx, you'll write to me?" '

ABOVE: *A cartoon to illustrate 'The Minx: A Poem in Prose' by Ada Leverson, which appeared in* Punch *in July 1894. This witty parody of Oscar Wilde's poem ended with the conclusion: 'Poet: In my opinion you are not a Sphinx at all. Sphinx (indignantly): What am I then? Poet: A Minx.' The illustration mimicked Ricketts' original cover design. '*Punch *is delightful and the drawing a masterpiece of caricature,' praised Wilde. 'I am afraid she really was a minx after all. You are the only Sphinx.'*

ABOVE: *Sir Alfred Wills, the 77-year-old presiding judge at Wilde's final trial. An expert on circumstantial evidence, his denunciation of Wilde in passing sentence was vehement: 'That you, Wilde, have been the centre of a circle of extensive corruption of the most hideous kind among young men, it is...impossible to doubt.'*

It was decided that Taylor was to be tried first. This was not helpful to Wilde's case. Edward Shelley took the stand against Wilde again – a new jury had been empanelled, so the evidence had to be raked through a second time – then a succession of servants from the Savoy Hotel testified, with an astonishing recall of detail from events two years previously, to suppers of cold fowl and champagne, boys in beds, and the inevitable stained bed linen. Wilde was again questioned about his friendship with Bosie – 'our friendship is founded on a rock,' he declared at one point – and again described his now notorious references to Bosie's rose-red lips 'made for the madness of kisses' as a 'decent...prose-poem' and not evidence of sensual love.

On the sixth day Mr Justice Wills summed up for the jury: 'There is some truth in the aphorism that a man must be judged by the company he keeps...you have seen the Parkers, you have seen Wood, and the same question must arise in your minds. Are these the kind of young men with whom you yourself would care to sit down and dine? Are these the sort of persons you would expect to find in the company of men of education?...'

The jury retired to consider its verdict. More than two hours later they returned: Wilde was guilty on all counts except 'the indictment relating to Edward Shelley'. Mr Justice Wills then addressed the dock:

Oscar Wilde and Alfred Taylor, the crime of which you have been convicted is so bad that one has to put stern restraint upon oneself to prevent oneself from describing, in language which I would rather not use, the sentiments which must rise to the breast of every man of honour who has heard the details of these two terrible trials...People who do these things must be dead to all sense of shame...It is the worst case I have ever tried...I shall, under such circumstances, be expected to pass the severest sentence that the law allows. In my judgement it is totally inadequate for such a case as this. The sentence of the Court is that each of you be imprisoned and kept to hard labour for two years.

ABOVE: *A sketch by Sir Robert Ponsoby-Staples of Edward Carson Q.C., 1898. Wilde's counsel did not participate in his last trial, which he did his best to prevent: 'Cannot you let up on the fellow now? He has suffered a great deal,' Carson pleaded with the Solicitor-General, Sir Frank Lockwood, after the jury had failed to agree on Wilde's guilt. 'I would but we cannot: we dare not: it would be said, both in England and abroad, that owing to the names... in Queensberry's letters we were forced to abandon it,' responded Lockwood.*

been dearer than you, never has any love been greater, more sacred, more beautiful…Every great love has its tragedy, and now ours has too, but to have known and loved you with such profound devotion, to have had for you a part of my life, the only part I now consider beautiful, is enough for me. My passion is at a loss for words, but you can understand me, you alone. …I think of you as a golden-haired boy with Christ's own heart in you. I know now how much greater love is than anything else…my sweet rose, my delicate flower, my lily of lilies, it is perhaps in prison that I am going to test the power of love.

But the love did not stand the test.

After my terrible sentence, when the prison-dress was on me, and the prison-house door closed, I sat amidst the ruins of my wonderful life, crushed by anguish, bewildered with terror, dazed through pain. But I would not hate you. Every day I said to myself, *I must keep Love in my heart today, else how shall I live through the day*. It did not occur to me then that you could have the supreme vice, shallowness.

The selfish shallowness of Lord Alfred Douglas had borne in on Oscar Wilde in his prison cell. While Bosie cavorted in France and Italy, Wilde grew thin and ill in his solitary humiliation, reflecting upon his life with Bosie and its torments and betrayals. He wrote out the lament for this life in the last months in Reading Gaol, to which he was transferred six months after his conviction. This was the ultimate moment of his 'public infamy'. On 20 November 1895 Wilde was obliged to:

> …stand on the centre platform of Clapham Junction in convict dress and handcuffed, for the world to look at…of all possible objects I was the most grotesque. When people saw me they laughed. Each train as it came in swelled the audience. Nothing could exceed their amusement….For half an hour I stood there in the grey November rain surrounded by a jeering mob. For a year after that was done to me I wept every day at the same time.

ABOVE: *A woodcut illustration by Franz Masereel for 'The Ballad of Reading Gaol':*

I never saw sad men who looked
With such a wistful eye…
at every happy cloud that passed
In such strange freedom by.

ABOVE: *A letter from the loyal Robert Ross requesting permission to visit Wilde, May 1896. In September 1895 Ross had waited to see Wilde at the Court of Bankruptcy, in order to raise his hat to him. 'Men have gone to heaven for smaller things than that,' wrote Wilde.*

Wilde's recollections on his relationship with Bosie had been given a particular force by a series of blows which fell within months of his imprisonment. Robert Sherard had been waiting for an opportunity to visit, which he eventually was granted in August: 'The ticket would have admitted another visitor, but though I wrote to different friends of his, I could find nobody to accompany me. Everybody was unfortunately engaged, but I was charged with many kind messages…' Sherard was later unable to remember much of the painful interview, except:

> the nerve shock that the rattle of the warder's keys and the clang of iron doors produced ….I noticed that his hands were disfigured, and that his nails were broken and bleeding; also that his head and face were untidy with growth of hair. He was greatly depressed, and at one time had tears in his eyes.

Sherard had learned that 'divorce proceedings were being urged upon [Constance]… if she abandoned him, his ruin would indeed be complete.'

Wilde had received a letter from Otho, Constance's brother, saying that 'if I would only write once to my wife she would, for my own sake and for my own children's sake, take no action for divorce. I felt my duty was to do so. Setting aside other reasons, I could not bear the idea of being separated from Cyril, that beautiful, loving, loveable child of mine….' Wilde accordingly wrote his wife 'a humble, penitent letter', considered by her solicitor to be 'the most touching and pathetic letter that had ever come under his eye'. Constance relented. 'Yesterday [Constance] wrote him a few lines to tell him there was forgiveness for him,' reported her brother Otho, who had changed his name, as had Constance and her sons, to Holland, 'and that Cyril never forgets him.' By the same post she wrote to the prison governor asking to be allowed a visit to Oscar. 'That she is acting for the best in taking him back…only time will tell,' Otho mused.

The second blow fell when a clerk from the Marquess of Queensberry's solicitor came to tell Wilde that his adversary had petitioned for him to be declared bankrupt; he was claiming the sum of £677, the costs of the

RIGHT (above and below): *The exterior and interior of Reading Gaol, to which Wilde was transferred to on 20 November 1895 to serve the remainder of his sentence. It had some 150 inmates an 'almost inhuman' governor, Major Isaacson. During his regime, the hanging of a soldier who had murdered his wife inspired Wilde's last poem 'The Ballad of Reading Gaol', written after his release. The arrival of a new governor, Major Nelson (the 'most Christ-like man' Wilde had ever met) much improved conditions at Reading Gaol.*

criminal libel case. Wilde was very bitter; it enflamed his hostility towards Douglas and the way in which Bosie's hate for his father had, he now decided, vivified his desire to revenge his own feelings, regardless of the cost to others:

I feel most strongly that these costs should have been borne by your family. You had taken personally on yourself the responsibility of stating that your family would do so. It was that which made the solicitor take up the case the way he did. You were absolutely responsible. You should have felt that, as you had brought the whole ruin on me, the least that could have been done was to spare me the additional ignominy of bankruptcy for an absolutely contemptible sum of money, less than half what I spent on you in three brief summer months.

News of the final twist of what Wilde now regarded as Bosie's treacherous selfishness came with Robert Sherard's second visit. Sherard told Wilde that he had 'heard from Paris' that Lord Alfred Douglas was planning to publish in 'that ridiculous *Mercure de France*, with its absurd affectation "an article" on me with specimens of my letters'. These were the private, passionate letters that Wilde had sent to Douglas during his trial:

My dearest boy, This is to assure you of my immortal, my eternal love for you. Tomorrow all will be over. If prison and dishonour be my destiny, think of my love for you and this idea, this still more divine belief, that you love me in return will sustain me in my unhappiness and will make me capable, I hope, of bearing my grief most patiently…I stretch out my hands towards you. Oh! may I live to touch your hair and your hands. I think that your love will watch over my life. If I should die, I want you to live a gentle, peaceful existence somewhere, with flowers, pictures, books, and lots of work. Dearest boy, sweetest of all young men, most loved and most loveable. Oh! wait for me! wait for me! I am now, as ever since the day we met, yours devoutly and with an immortal love   Oscar.

LEFT: *A photograph of Wilde's eldest son Cyril that illustrated an article in* The Studio *art magazine in 1893. 'I could not bear the idea of being separated from Cyril, that beautiful, loving, loveable child of mine,' wrote Wilde to Bosie. Cyril and his younger brother, Vyvyan, were taken abroad by their mother after their father's conviction and their surname changed to Holland. Although Constance did not not wish them to forget Oscar ('Try not to feel harshly about your father; remember that he is your father and that he loves you,' she wrote to Cyril), Wilde was never to see his children again.*

The
Ballad of Reading Gaol
By
C. 3. 3.

Leonard Smithers
Royal Arcade London W
Mdcccxcviii

ABOVE: *The title page of 'The Ballad of Reading Gaol', published on hand-made paper in February 1898 by Leonard Smithers. Wilde's previous publisher, John Lane, declined the work of the now disgraced author, who was identified by his cell number at Reading, C.3.3. The work was a success for Smithers, who always boasted 'I'll publish anything that the others are afraid of'; it sold in thousands.*

It had been two earlier letters from Wilde to Bosie that had provided the evidence for Queensberry's defence in the libel case – and had thus led to Wilde's present predicament. Now Bosie was proposing to enflame the matter further by publishing Wilde's letters from Holloway, letters 'that should have been to you things sacred and secret beyond anything in the world!...for the jaded *décadent* to wonder at'. These were missives which would demonstrate that he had perjured himself in the witness box and could do nothing but harm to Wilde's already fragile relations with his wife and family. It was all undertaken for some vain idea of Bosie's self-justification, which Wilde now saw as self-aggrandizement and utter, vain foolishness. His feelings of betrayal were complete. When Constance visited him – a visit that was 'indeed awful,' she told Sherard, 'more so than I had any conception it could be... I could not see him and I could not touch him. I scarcely spoke' – Wilde told her that 'he has been mad these last three years, and he says that if he saw Alfred Douglas he would kill him. So he had better keep away and be satisfied with having marred a fine life. Few people can boast of so much.'

Later in Cell C.3.3 at Reading Gaol as he recognized that, whilst for him 'the beautiful world of colour and motion has been taken away', Bosie 'walked free among the flowers,' he wrote the savage indictment of their love, later known as *De Profundis*. In this letter, Wilde's bitterness took excoriating voice:

> I...had my illusions. I thought life was going to be a brilliant comedy, and that you were going to be one of the many graceful figures in it. I found it to be a revolting and repellent tragedy...you can now understand – can you not? – a little of what I am suffering...the memory of our friendship is the shadow that walks with me here: that never seems to leave me: that wakes me up at night to tell me the same story over and over till its wearisome iteration makes all sleep abandon me till dawn: at dawn it begins again: it follows me into the prison-yard and makes me talk to myself as I tramp round: each detail that

ABOVE: *A woodcut illustration of prisoner C.3.3. (Wilde) by Franz Masereel. It was produced for a 1924 edition of 'The Ballad of Reading Gaol'.*

That every prison that men build
Is built with bricks of shame
And bound with bars lest Christ should see
How men their brothers maim.

accompanied each dreadful moment I am forced to recall…The gods are strange…it is not of our vices only they make instruments to scourge us. They bring us to ruin through what in us is good, gentle, humane, loving. But for my pity and affection for you and yours, I would not now be weeping in this terrible place.

On 19 February 1896 Constance travelled from Genoa in Italy, where she was now living with her children, to visit Reading Gaol. She was the bearer of bad news: rather than let him hear it from 'indifferent or alien lips', she had come to tell him of his mother's death. Speranza had requested on her death bed that her son might be allowed out to see her: the request was turned down. Oscar was devastated:

> Her death was so terrible to me that I, once lord of language, have no words in which to express my anguish and my shame…she and my father had bequeathed me a name they had made noble and honoured not merely in Literature, Art, Archaeology and Science, but in the public history of my own country in its evolution as a nation. I had disgraced that name eternally. I had made it a low byword among low people. I had dragged it through the very mire. I had given it to brutes that they might make it brutal, and to fools that they might turn it into a synonym for folly. What I suffered then, and still suffer, is not for pen to write or paper to record.

This was the last time Oscar and his wife were to meet: 'She was gentle and good to me,' recalled Oscar. Financial arrangements were agreed which led finally to Constance settling an allowance of £150 per year on her husband, providing that he did nothing that would cause his wife to divorce him or to seek a judicial separation, was not guilty of any moral misconduct and did not 'notoriously consort with evil or disreputable persons'. Unknown to Wilde, Constance accompanied her solicitor to Reading Gaol when the agreement was signed and asked to have 'one last look' at her husband. The

ABOVE: *A page of the manuscript for* De Profundis, *Wilde's searing 'letter' to Bosie, which he wrote in his last three months in Reading Gaol after the new governor had allowed him a continual supply of writing materials. Wilde advised Douglas to 'read this letter over and over again until it kills your vanity'. In fact Bosie was not to read the letter addressed to himself in full until 1912.*

In Memoriam

JANE FRANCESCA AGNES SPERANZA,
LADY WILDE,
Widow of Sir William Wilde, M.D.,
SURGEON OCULIST TO THE QUEEN IN IRELAND, KNIGHT OF THE ORDER
OF THE NORTH STAR IN SWEDEN.
*Died at her residence, 146, Oakley Street,
Chelsea, London, Feb. 3rd, 1896.*

LEFT *(above): A photograph of Lady Wilde in old age. Speranza was adamant that Wilde should stay and face trial. 'If you stay, even if you go to prison, you will always be my son. It will make no difference to my affection. But if you go, I will never speak to you again,' she told him. He stayed, and she died whilst he was in prison.*

LEFT *(below): The black-edged card announcing the death of Lady Wilde. Oscar was devastated by the news, which he heard in prison from Constance.*

LEFT: Vernet's Dieppe *by Walter Sickert. Vernet's was a popular café-chantant on the Dieppe quayside, a centre of activity by day and night. Wilde's first destination on leaving Reading was Dieppe, a fashionable resort in France in the 1890s. Wilde had met Sickert and was friendly with his sister Helena (whom he addressed in letters as 'Miss Nellie'); he had also been kind to Sickert's mother at the time of his father's death. However, Walter Sickert was pointedly to shun Wilde's company when he saw him in exile in Dieppe.*

warder outside his cell stepped aside to enable Constance to peer through the spy hole as Wilde signed the document of agreement. He did not see her, and she left the prison 'apparently labouring under deep emotion'. His family was sundered. Already 'my two children [were] taken from me by legal procedure. That is and always will remain to me a source of infinite distress, of infinite pain, of grief without limit.'

Oscar Wilde was released from prison in the early morning of 19 May 1897. He had served the full two years of his sentence to the day. The last weeks had been spent fussing about his release. 'I was mentally upset and in a state of very terrible nervous excitement.' Where was his fur coat 'my two rugs, one fur rug, the other a travelling rug: two portmanteaus, one brown leather with my initials, the other black: my large double hat-box?' Had they been pawned? He requested 'if there is time, get me *eighteen* collars made after the pattern you have, or say two dozen. I want for psychological reasons, to feel entirely physically cleansed of the stain and soil of prison life, so these things are all – trivial as they may sound – really of great importance.'

There was, of course, the question of money. Frank Harris 'had made a very large sum of money – some £23,000 in South Africa' and volunteered to put his cheque book at Wilde's disposal, but then changed his mind after all. Percy Douglas's parsimony showed that he was:

bien le fils de son père. One of the notes about the Queensberry family is that they are quite unscrupulous about money affairs and extremely mean about them…I loathe promise makers. I could be humble and grateful to a beggar who gave me half a crust out of his wallet, but the rich, the ostentatious and the false …I have nothing but contempt for them…If anyone comes to you with promises and offers of help for me, tell them to give what they can – if it be a piece of bread I could thank them – but don't let them promise anything. I won't have any more *promises*. People think that because one is in prison they can treat one as they choose…

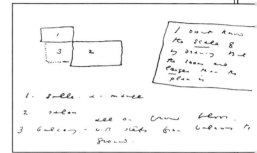

ABOVE: *A sketch of the church at Berneval Le Grand containing the shrine of Notre Dame de Liesse. 'I always wanted to be a pilgrim,' wrote Wilde to Ross on 31 May 1897, 'and I …start early tomorrow at the shrine of Notre Dame de Liesse…an old word for joy…Need I say that this is a miracle? I find this little grey stone chapel of Our Lady of Joy is brought to me.*

ABOVE: *Wilde's ground floor plan for a chalet in Berneval. He liked the surrounding area and toyed with having a chalet built to his specifications. His friend Robert Ross pointed out the financial obstacles and predicted that Wilde would soon feel the lure of Paris again.*

RIGHT: *The official Diamond Jubilee
photograph of Queen Victoria, 1897.
Wilde organized a celebration of this
event for some Dieppe children, which,
as he wrote to Bosie, proved a huge success:
'fifteen* gamins *were entertained on
strawberries and cream, apricots,
chocolates, cakes and* sirop de
grenadine*…They sang the Marseillaise
and other songs, and danced a* ronde,
*and also played "God save the Queen"
… I gave the health of* La reine
d'Angleterre!!!!*…Then* Le Président
de la République*…they cried out with
one accord "* Vivent le Président de la
République et Monsieur Melmoth"!!!
*…So I found my name coupled with that
of the President. It was an amusing
experience as I am hardly more than a
month out of gaol.'*

Finally there was the question of where to go. 'I now hear that Dieppe has
been decided on. I dislike it as I am so well known there, but I can move
on I suppose.' Wilde wrote to Reggie Turner, whom he had asked to meet
him from prison: 'I daresay a handsome would do, but a little brougham
with blinds might be best…and engage a first-class carriage [on the boat
train] in any name you chose – *Mr Melmoth* is my name: so let it be that.'
So C.3.3 went into exile as Sebastian Melmoth. It was a carefully chosen
alias. Paintings of the martyr St Sebastian were among the works of art
Wilde most admired; 'fair as Sebastian and as early slain', he had written
in his ode on Keats' Grave in 1877. His great uncle, Charles Maturin, had
written a novel *Melmoth the Wanderer*, published in 1820.

The ex-convict was driven to the house in Bloomsbury of the Revd.
Stuart Headlam, a Socialist clergyman of private means and high principles
who had stood bail for Wilde in 1895, believing that his case had been
judged before it came to court. Ada Leverson, with her husband Ernest,
whom Wilde had accused to his friends of having 'taken' the money
entrusted to him to pay Wilde's creditors, were also there to greet him that
'cold May morning'. Ada Leverson recalled the friends' embarrassment:

> We had an English fear of showing our feelings, and at the same time the
> human fear of not showing our feelings. [Wilde] at once put us at our
> ease…he came in with the dignity of a king returning from exile. he came in
> talking, laughing, smoking a cigarette, with waved hair and a flower in his
> button-hole, and he looked markedly better, slighter and younger than he
> had two years previously. His first words were 'Sphinx, how marvellous of
> you to know exactly the right hat to wear at seven o'clock in the morning to
> meet a friend who has been away!'

Wilde's request to enter a Roman Catholic retreat having been turned
down, he left to catch the boat train from Newhaven to Dieppe. Arriving
in Dieppe at 4am, he walked down the pier with his 'odd elephantine gait'
to where Reggie Turner and Robert Ross stood waiting for the exile.

ABOVE: *'I have a bathing costume for you here, but you had better get one in Paris. Also bring me lots of books, and cigarettes...Bring also some perfumes and nice things from the sellers of the dust of roses. Also bring yourself...' Less than a month after leaving prison, Wilde was once again writing love letters to Bosie, 'cause of my disgrace'.*

Wilde's friends had managed to raise £800 for him: Constance had sent money too and Wilde rejoiced in his customary way in his freedom. 'Robbie detected me in the market place of the sellers of perfumes, spending all my money on orris-root and the tears of the narcissus and the dust of red roses. He was very stern and led me away. I have already spent my entire income for two years.'

'The cruelty of a prison sentence starts when you come out,' wrote Wilde. His wilderness years were to be pre-occupied with Bosie, his children, the iniquities of the prison system — and the inevitable money: 'like dear St Francis of Assisi I am wedded to poverty, but in my case the marriage is not a success. I hate the bride that has been given to me.'

From Dieppe he went along the coast to Berneval which he soon 'felt to be home. I really do,' and where he took a chalet. Missing his friends, he 'was forced to write poetry. I have begun something that I think will be very good.' This was *The Ballad of Reading Gaol*, ostensibly the story of Charles Woolridge, a trooper in the Royal Horse Guards who had been sentenced to death for the murder of his wife. On 7 July 1896 Wilde had seen the hangman crossing the yard to his scaffold, and the poem he was to write was an indictment of man's inhumanity to man, both as Wilde had experienced it himself and as it was codified by the British penal system:

> *I know not whether Laws be right,*
> *Or whether Laws be wrong;*
> *All that we know who lie in gaol*
> *Is that the wall is strong;*
> *And that each day is like a year,*
> *A year whose days are long.*

The *Ballad* was 'written from personal experience, a sort of denial of my own philosophy of art in many ways. I hope it is good...' However, there

ABOVE: *An illustration of the Chalet Bourgeat, Wilde's rented home in Berneval, from* After Reading, *a collection of letters from Wilde to Ross. Wilde wrote of Berneval; 'I adore this place. The whole country is lovely, and full of forest and deep meadow...if I lived in Egypt I know what my life would be. If I lived in the south of Italy I know I should be idle, and worse. I want to live here...'*

was to be no more writing. As Wilde wrote to Ross, 'I don't think I shall ever write again. Something is killed in me. I feel no desire to write. I am unconscious of power. Of course my first year in prison destroyed me. It could not have been otherwise.'

But what neither prison nor the supposedly cathartic exercise of writing could do was to break Wilde of the ties that still inextricably bound him to Bosie. Constance had made it a condition of her husband's allowance that he should not resume his relationship with Lord Alfred Douglas: Lady Queensberry had made it a condition of her allowance to her son that he should keep away from Wilde. Wilde had felt 'too weak' on his release from prison to entertain the thought of a visit – 'keep Bosie away at all costs,' he instructed his friends. But Bosie bombarded Wilde with letters. Wilde replied in equal number: 'in the old adoring strain' – soon it was 'My darling Boy' again. Wilde admitted that he knew Bosie was 'a gilded pillar of infamy', but three months after his release from gaol the two were reunited at the Hôtel de la Poste in Rouen on 24 August 1898. They wept, held hands, and Wilde admitted that 'Everyone is furious with me for going back to you, but they don't understand us'. He pledged 'It is only with you that I can do anything at all. Do remake my ruined life for me, and then our friendship and love will have a different meaning to the world.'

But that Bosie could not, and finally would not, do. The lovers travelled to Naples, where Wilde bitterly told Bosie that he, surely he, should know what the recurrent words of the *Ballad* meant:

> All men kill the thing they love...
> The coward does it with a kiss
> The brave man with a sword!

The treadmill of a destructive passion had started again, with inevitable results. In a letter to Ross Wilde wrote:

BELOW: *A photograph of Oscar Wilde standing outside St Peter's in Rome. 'Rome has quite absorbed me,' he confessed to Robert Ross on 14 May 1900, 'I must winter here; it is the only city of the soul.'*

ABOVE: *An illustration of the Bay of Naples from* After Berneval. *'How can you keep on asking if Lord Alfred Douglas is in Naples? You know quite well he is,' Wilde reprimanded Leonard Smithers in October 1897. 'We are together. He understands me and my art, and loves both. I hope never to be separated from him. He is witty, graceful, lovely to look at, loveable to be with. He has also ruined my life, so I can't help loving him — it is the only thing to do.'*

LEFT: Oscar Wilde au cabaret, Rue de Dunkerque, *a sketch by Jean Matet. 'Is there any chance of your being in Paris?' the lonely Wilde asked Leonard Smithers in September 1900. 'My dear Neapolitans have returned to Naples and I miss that brown faun with his deep woodland eyes and his sensuous grace of limb. A slim brown Eygptian, rather like a handsome bamboo walking-stick, occasionally serves me drinks at the Café d'Egypt, but he does not console me for the the loss of the wanton sylvan boy of Italy...'*

Bosie, for four months, by endless letters, offered me a 'home'. He offered me love, affection and care, and promised that I should never want for anything. After four months I accepted his offer, but, when we met...I found he had no money, no plans, and had forgotten all his promises. His one idea was that I should raise money for us both. I did so, to the extent of £120. On this, Bosie lived, quite happily. When it came to his having, of course, to repay his own *share*, he became terrible, unkind, mean, and penurious except where his own pleasures were concerned, and when my allowance ceased, he left… It is, of course, the most bitter experience of a bitter life…

There were others. Constance consistently refused to see Wilde or to let him see his sons, though she sent photographs of them 'looking so sweet in their Eton collars'. She had also written with unusual vehemence 'I *forbid* you to see Lord Alfred Douglas. I forbid you to return to your filthy, insane life...I forbid you to come to Genoa.' On 12 April 1898 Wilde sent a stark telegram to Robert Ross: 'Constance is dead...Am in great grief'. Constance had been ill for some time; she died, aged forty, of paralysis of the spine, caused in the first place by a fall at Tite Street. Wilde's allowance was now unconditional. Constance in death, as in life, was ready to forgive Oscar anything.

Nevertheless, money continued to be a pressing problem. Some friends, like Will Rothenstein, tried to help; others, such as Aubrey Beardsley and Walter Sickert, artists who both had reason to return Wilde's earlier kindnesses to them, shunned and wounded him. He made some new friends, like the poet of decadence Ernest Dowson, but most of his acquaintances in the end recoiled from his incessant demands for money. Bosie was, significantly, of little assistance. The American writer, Vincent O'Sullivan, who knew Wilde in Paris at this time, recalled:

Physical loneliness he could not stand, and so to avoid it he seized any measures that offered. So he did take to frequenting a little bar on the Boulevard des Italiens...there he could always find someone to talk to, were it only the bar tender...what was he to do? The censorious took care not to invite him to their houses...he went to places like the Kalisaya driven by the instinct of self-preservation. He knew he would go mad if he sat alone with his bitter thoughts. Besides, where was he to sit? In the room of his hotel with the thousand noises of the cheap hotel? As well be back in his prison cell...But for his moral lonlieness there was no remedy bad or good.

ABOVE: *The unpaid Paris hotel bill, in the name of Mr Melmoth, which had to be settled after Wilde's death. Wilde had asked Frank Harris for money for this purpose in September 1900: 'Could you send me £20? I am quite without a sou, and I must give the landlord £15.' He observed bitterly to Alice Rothenstein 'I can't even afford to die'.*

ABOVE: *A sketch showing the Rue des Beaux-Arts in Paris, where Wilde's final hotel, the Hôtel d'Alsace, was located.*

153

RIGHT: Maison dans la Cour *from Quelques aspects de la vie de Paris by Pierre Bonnard, 1899. Wilde's lodgings at the Hôtel d'Alsace would have given the invalid a similar view. His illness grew worse through October and November 1900; Reginald Turner was to write in anxiety to Ross on 26 November: 'Oscar is not in want of anything...as he is not sensible enough to desire anything. The* patron *is awfully good to him, but a bit of a bore. You had better write to Bosie, I think...Oscar has not asked for anyone and I don't think realises any danger...ought he to have a priest or Protestant clergyman if he gets worse? If he is at the last gasp could you come to Paris?' Wilde died in the hotel on 30 November.*

The father of the writer Graham Greene met him in Naples in the spring of 1898; Wilde talked for an hour and left Greene and his companion to pay for his drinks, having paid himself 'in the only currency he had'.

It was not an existence that could be endured for long. Wilde developed a severe ear infection, undergoing an unsuccessful operation in his hotel room in October 1900. In November, Reggie Turner sent Robert Ross a telegram: 'Almost Hopeless', it read. Ross raced to Paris and arrived at the Hôtel d'Alsace, where the proprietor was 'a most charitable and humane man [who] never spoke to Mr Wilde on the subject of his debt …[and] paid himself for luxuries and necessities ordered by the physicians'. Wilde was, in his own words, 'dying beyond his means'.

At ten minutes to two in the afternoon of 30 November 1900 Oscar Wilde died, fortified by the rites of the Roman Catholic church into which he had been received on his death bed. His loyal friends Reggie Turner and Robert Ross were with him at the end. Lord Alfred Douglas 'rushed over to Paris…[but] he was already in his nailed-up coffin by the time…I arrived…I acted as chief mourner at his funeral in the beautiful church of Saint Germain-des-Prés and followed his hearse to the grave.'

'I suppose it was better that Oscar should die,' Wilde's old friend Max Beerbohm wrote to Turner. 'If he had lived to be an old man he would have become unhappy. Those whom the gods, etc. And the gods *did* love Oscar with all his faults…'

Wilde's final resting place is the cemetery of Père Lachaise in Paris. His tomb, which features a monument designed by Jacob Epstein, bears an inscription from *The Ballad of Reading Gaol*:

> *And alien tears will fill for him*
> *Pity's long broken urn*
> *For his mourners will be outcast men*
> *And outcasts always mourn.*

ABOVE: *A photograph of Robert Ross in 1911, reading an edition of Wilde's apologia, De Profundis. Wilde had handed him the manuscript on his release from prison, and Ross, who was to be his literary executor, arranged for the publication of extracts in 1905. Ross proved himself to be the most loyal of all Wilde's friends, as Wilde recognised in a letter from Berneval in 1897: 'I couldn't spoil your life by accepting the sweet companionship you offer me from time to time. It is not for nothing that I named you in prison St Robert of Phillimore [the London square where Ross lived]. Love can canonise people. The saints are those who have been most loved…'*

ABOVE: *The death certificate of Oscar Wilde, whose doctors had diagnosed cerebral meningitis on 27 November. It was, of course, Turner and Ross who had to cope with the administrative complexities their friend's demise unleashed: 'While Reggie stayed at the hotel interviewing journalists and clamorous creditors, I started, with Gesling, to see officials. We did not part till 1.30, so you can imagine the formalities and oaths and exclamations and signing of papers. Dying in Paris is really a very difficult and expensive luxury for a foreigner.'*

Florence Balcombe (1858–1937) Oscar Wilde's first love whom he met in Dublin in August 1875 when she was 17 and he was 20. The daughter of a retired lieutenant-colonel, Florrie was considered by George du Maurier to be one of the three most beautiful women he had ever seen. She married the drama critic Bram Stoker (who later wrote *Dracula*) in 1878.

Aubrey Beardsley (1872–98) Artist and illustrator, he did the drawings for *Salome* (1894) and was art editor of *The Yellow Book* between 1894–5. He converted to Roman Catholicism and died of TB at the age of 25.

Max Beerbohm (Henry Maximillian Beerbohm)(1872–1956) Caricaturist, essayist and author of *Zuleika Dobson* (1911). Met Wilde in 1888 whilst was still at school, and, as an undergraduate at Oxford, he contributed a controversial article on cosmetics to the first issue of *The Yellow Book*. Beerbohm caricatured himself, Wilde (often pointedly) and most of his circle.

Sarah Bernhardt (1844–1923) The 'great Bernhardt', who lived much of her life in England, was the most glamorous and illustrious actress of her generation. She stormed the London stage in Racine's *Phèdre*; her greatest triumph was as Marguerite in *La Dame aux Camélias*, but she was probably best known for her parts in Sardou's melodramas, including *Fédora* (which Wilde saw in Paris in 1883). She was rehearsing in Wilde's *Salome* when it was banned by the censor. Despite his hope that she would one day do so, Bernhardt never appeared in one of Wilde's plays.

Lord Alfred Douglas ('Bosie') (1870–1945) Third son of the eighth Marquess of Queensberry, he met Wilde in 1891 whilst an undergraduate at Oxford. He translated *Salome* into English and published poetry; he was also the fatal passion of Wilde's life and the subject and object of *De Profundis*. After Wilde's death Douglas wrote several books giving his perceptions of his relationship with Wilde.

Frank Harris (1856–1931) Author, editor and adventurer. Harris spent much of his youth in America, returning to England in 1881 to edit the *Evening News*. He was appointed editor of the *Fortnightly Review* in 1886 and in 1894 bought the *Saturday Review* in which Wilde's aphorisms 'A Few Maxims for the Instruction of the Over-Educated' first appeared anonymously. He made an appearance at key points in Wilde's life and remained steadfast – if not always appreciated – until the end. Wilde said of him 'Frank Harris has no feelings. It is the secret of his success.' His biography of Wilde, first published in 1916, is factually fanciful at times, but probably impressionistically accurate and certainly vivid.

Lillie Langtry (1852–1929) Society beauty and would-be actress. Born Emilie Louise Le Breton in the Channel Islands, Langtry was painted by Whistler, Poynter Watts, Burne-Jones, Leighton and Millais (from whose picture she took the nickname 'The Jersey Lilly'). She became the mistress of the Prince of Wales and a close friend and occasional muse of Wilde in his early days in London.

Ada Leverson (1862–1933) Novelist and journalist. Born Ada Beddington, she married Ernest Leverson, son of a diamond merchant. Wilde admired her wit, calling her his 'Sphinx' she proved a loyal friend, giving him sanctuary whilst he was on bail and meeting him on his release.

Walter Pater (1839–94) Fellow and Tutor of Brasenose College, Oxford, when Wilde was a student at Magdalen. Pater's *Studies in the History of the Renaissance* (1873), which established his reputation as a moving spirit of the aesthetic movement, was Wilde's 'golden book'; he could quote long passages verbatim, and he requested a copy among his limited reading matter when in prison. Pater coined the aesthete's slogan 'Art for Art's sake', and his best-known book *Marius the Epicurean* (1885) was a major influence on the aesthetic ideal of artistic individuality.

Oscar Wilde and his circle

Queensberry, Marquess of (1844–1900) John Sholto Douglas, Eighth Marquess. Father of Lord Alfred Douglas and a pugilist who gave his name to the 'Queensberry rules' for boxing in 1867. His harassment and alleged libel of Wilde led to Wilde's conviction and imprisonment in 1895.

Charles Ricketts (1866–1931) Artist, writer, book and stage designer who, with his lifelong companion Charles Shannon, (1863-1937) was responsible for the design and decoration of many of Wilde's works including *The Picture of Dorian Gray, Intentions, The Sphinx, The House of Pomegranates*, and the plays. They also ran a privately printed magazine of the arts, *The Dial*, between 1889 and 1897.

Robert Ross (1869 1918) Literary journalist and art critic. 'Robbie' Ross – who had 'a face like Puck' – was the grandson of the first prime minister of Canada. He met Wilde in 1886, becoming probably his first lover and certainly his friend for life – and beyond. He attended Wilde's trial, visited him in prison and in exile and was present at his deathbed. He became Wilde's literary executor and arranged for the publication of extracts from *De Profundis* in 1905 – none of which mentioned Bosie.

John Ruskin (1819–1900) Slade Professor of Fine Art at Oxford. Wilde attended his famed lectures on Florentine Art in 1874 and, after a visit to Italy himself, became a friend and disciple of Ruskin, author of 39 works including *The Seven Lamps of Architecture* (1849) and *The Stones of Venice*. (1851 3). Ruskin's view of the artist's moral role to educate his viewers to revere divine creation was also an indictment of Victorian materialism. In the latter part of the 19th century his social criticism increasingly became the focus of his work and influence on the arts.

Reginald Turner (1869–1938) Journalist and novelist. Possibly the illegitimate son of Lord Burnham, the proprietor/editor of the *Daily Telegraph*, or of his brother, and a lifelong friend of Max Beerbohm, he became part of Wilde's circle. It was Turner who took charge of Wilde's dying: 'He had the worst time of all in many ways,' acknowledged Ross.

James McNeill Whistler (1834–1903) American artist who studied in Paris and lived mainly in London. Wilde greatly admired his French-influenced art, which was a reproach to Victorian realist painting. Wilde and Whistler were similar as *flâneurs*, dandies, wits and theorists about art, artists and critics. Consequently they were also competitors; their views about art diverged and their repartee grew more barbed, particularly on Whistler's part. By 1890 Wilde features in Whistler's book, *The Gentle Art of Making Enemies,* as one of them.

Constance Wilde (née Lloyd) (1857–98). Wife of Oscar Wilde and mother of his two sons. From a distinguished Irish legal family, she married Wilde in London on 29 May 1884. After his conviction and imprisonment, Constance fled abroad with the children and changed the family name to Holland. She died after an operation in Genoa for a spinal injury she had sustained by falling down the stairs at Tite Street some years earlier.

Lady Wilde (1821–96) Mother of Oscar Wilde, born Jane Francesca Elgee, granddaughter of an Archdeacon from Co. Wexford in Ireland. Took the name of 'Speranza' (Italian for 'hope') as a pseudonym for her Irish nationalist journalism and poetry.

Sir William Wilde (1815–76) Father of Oscar Wilde. An eminent Irish ophthalmic and aural surgeon, medical statistician, archaeologist, historian and folklorist, he was knighted in 1864.

Index

INDEX

ACKNOWLEDGEMENTS

There are many fine works on the life and writings of Oscar Wilde spanning this entire century and only their existence made it possible for me to write this one. I am particularly indebted to the following books for information, insights and great interest.

Wherever possible I have tried to use Oscar Wilde's own words and for this reason and many others I am particularly grateful to Rupert Hart-Davis and Merlin Holland for permission to quote from *The Letters of Oscar Wilde* (Rupert Hart-Davis, 1962) and *More Letters of Oscar Wilde* (John Murray, 1985,) as well as drawing on Rupert Hart-Davis' extensive editorial notes in both editions. Richard Ellmann's *Oscar Wilde* (Hamish Hamilton, 1987) is the fullest life possible and anyone writing anything about Wilde since its publication is beholden to its scholarship and illumination. (But see also Horst Schroeder *Additions and Corrections to Richard Ellmann's 'Oscar Wilde'*,1989). The biographies of Wilde by Rupert Croft-Cook (1972); Vyvyan Holland (1960); H. Montgomery Hyde (1975 – also *The Trials of Oscar Wilde* (1948 new ed. 1962 and *The Aftermath*, 1975); Hesketh Pearson (1946) and the memoirs, diaries and collected letters of those who knew Wilde are of course essential sources. These include: Aubrey Beardsley (1970); Max Beerbohm (1972); David Hunter Blair (1939); Wilfred Scawen Blunt (1919); Lord Alfred Douglas (1909, 1914, 1929,1934 and 1962); Ernest Dowson (1967); André Gide (1938); Charles and Edmond de Goncourt (1962 trans.); Frank Harris (1915 and1930); Vyvyan Holland (1954); A.E. Housman (1971); Lillie Langtry (1925); Ada Leverson (1930); Charles Ricketts (with Jean Paul Raymond, 1932); Rennell Rodd (1922); Robert Ross (1952); William Rothenstein (1931); Robert H. Sherard (1902, 1906 and 1917); Mrs H.M. Swanwick (Helena Sickert, 1935); James Mc Neill Whistler (1890) and W.B. Yeats (1965). *Oscar Wilde Discovers America* by Lloyd Lewis and Henry Justin Smith is visually as well as textually fascinating as are the relevant issues of *Artist and Journal of Home Culture*, *Pall Mall Gazette*, *Punch*, *Studio*, *Woman's World* and *The Yellow Book*. The 15-volume *Sunflower Edition* of Oscar Wilde's works was published in 1909; Wm. Collins edition of *The Complete Works of Oscar Wilde* in 1966; Ian Small, *Oscar Wilde Revalued: An Essay on New Materials and Methods of Research* in 1993 and Norman Page *An Oscar Wilde Chronology* in 1991. Recent scholarship has added considerably to an understanding and appreciation of Wilde. Neil Bartlett, *Who Was That Man? A Present for Mr Oscar Wilde* (1988); Karl Beckson *London in the 1890s: A Cultural History* (1990); Patricia Behrendt, *Oscar Wilde: Eros and Aesthetics* (1992); Ed Cohen, *Talk on the Wilde Side* (1992); Richard Dellmora, *Masculine Desire: The Sexual Politics of Victorian Aestheticism* (1990); Jonathan Dollimore, *Sexual Dissidence* (1991); Regenia Gagnier, *Idylls of the Marketplace: Oscar Wilde and the Victorian Public* (1986); Norbert Kohl, *Oscar Wilde: The Work of a Conformist Rebel* (1980); Brian Reade, *Sexual Heretics: Male Homosexuality in English Literature from 1850 to 1900 : An Anthology*; (1970); Elanie Showalter *Sexual Anarchy* (1992); Gary Schmidgall, *The Stranger Wilde* (1994).

I would also like to acknowledge -and thank – the enthusiasm, support and careful patience of my editor, Catherine Bradley: the valuable work of Philippa Lewis in picture research, Ruth Prentice in design and Susan Martineau in copy-editing. I would also like to thank Merlin Holland for his kind assistance on this project.

The illustrations are reproduced by kind permission of the following:
Art Resource/Giraudon 51; Ashmolean Museum, Oxford 140; Birmingham Museum & Art Gallery 27; Bridgeman Art Library 2, 34, 87, 91, 114, 119, 134 left, 147; British Library 146 left; Musée Carnavalet (photo Lauros-Giraudon/Bridgeman Art Library) 63-64 Christie's Images 23, 28 left, 60 right, 120, 130, 155; Detroit Institute of Arts (photo Bridgeman Art Library) 82; Mary Evans Picture Library 108, 126, 127; Fine Art Photographs 94,107; Fotomas 25; John Frost Historical Newspaper Service 132 left, 141; University of Hull Art Collection 101; Hulton Deutsch Collection 32, 76, 80, 99, 129, 132 right, 139 left, 151 left; Hunterian Art Gallery, University of Glasgow, Birnie Philip Bequest 86 right, 116; James Hunter Blairquhan (photo Christine Ottewill) 29; Leeds City Art Gallery 66; Mander & Mitchenson Theatre Collection 7, 22, 42 left, 43, 48, 62, 100, 103 top and left, 104, 106, 111, 112, 122 left, 123; Mansell Collection 21, 28 right, 33, 54, 60 left, 61, 69 left, 96, 103 right, 136, 149; Warden & Fellows of Merton College, Oxford 96; David Messum Fine Art 72, 122 right; National Gallery of Ireland 10-11, 14 right, 15, 16-17, 19, 67, 102; National Portrait Gallery 31, 139 right, 154 left; Oxfordshire Photographic Archive 24-25, 26, 36; Private Collection (photo Fine Art Society, London) 135; The Pope Family Trust (photo Bridgeman Art Library) 38-39; Portora Royal School, Enniskillen 16; The Public Record Office 125; Range Pictures/Bettman Archive 46 left, 49, 52, 53, 55, 56, 57, 58, 59 left; Reading Central Library 143; James Robertson (photo Michael Newton) 86 left; Roger-Viollet, Paris 9, 35, 64, 118, 152; Sotheby & Co. 40, 78; Amoret Tanner Ephemera Collection 50, 75, 98; Tate Gallery 6, 30, 46, 74, 92, 109, 115 right; Topham Picturepoint 93, 128, 133; The Borad of Trinity College, Dublin 20; Usher Art Gallery, Lincoln 90 left; Victoria & Albert Museum 41, 42 right, 62, 70, 71, 90 right; Francis Wyndham 138 left; Yale University Art Gallery (photo Bridgeman Art Library) 47. *These illustrations come from the following books and periodicals*: Max Beerbohm, *Caricatures of Twenty-five Gentlemen*, 1896: 73, 113, 115 left, 121, 131; *Home Notes*, edited by 'Isobel', 1894: 75; William Rothenstein, *Oxford Characters*, 1896: 24; R.H.Sherard, *The Life of Oscar Wilde*, 1906: 13, 117, 146 bottom, 154 right; R.H.Sherard, *The Real Oscar Wilde*, 1917: 12 right, 38, 68, 142 right, 146 top; *The Studio*, vol. 1, 1893: 85, 134 right, 144; J.M.Whistler, *The Gentle Art of Making Enemies*, 1890: 82 right, 87 right, William Wilde, *The Beauties of the Boyne and Blackwater*, 1850: 11, 14 left, 16-17 top; Oscar Wilde, *After Reading*:(letters to Robert Ross), 1921: 148, 150 right; Oscar Wilde, *After Berneval*: (letters to Robert Ross), 1922: 151 right, 153 right, *The Woman's World*, edited by Oscar Wilde, 1888: 75, 77. *Front jacket*: Oscar Wilde by Henri de Toulouse-Lautrec, Bridgeman Art Library; Letter and photograph, Christie's Images; Programme for *The Importance of Being Earnest*, Mander & Mitchenson Theatre Collection; detail from American trade card, Amoret Tanner Ephemera Collection. *Back jacket*: Detail from *A Private View at the Royal Academy*, 1881, by W.P.Frith, The Pope Family Trust, Bridgeman Art Library. *Frontispiece*: *Danse de la Goulue* by Henri de Toulouse-Lautrec, Musee d'Orsay, Paris (Bridgeman Art Library).